THE DARK PSYCHOLOGY

BLUEPRINT

BY

KYLE MURPHY
&
ROSS DAVIS

TABLE OF CONTENTS

HOW TO ANALYZE PEOPLE 101

THE UNKNOWN SCIENCE OF DARK PSYCHOLOGY

HOW TO ANALYZE PEOPLE 101

101

BY

ROSS DAVIS

INTRODUCTION

Throughout the years, analyzing people as I approach them has been so easy for me. I see it as a skill, although it's just something that I accidentally learned throughout my teenage years when I started working at a restaurant as a server – I would look at people who enter the facility and guess what would they order, how much they would spend, and how they would treat the staff – I was almost always correct, and throughout the years, it just developed. Yes, I know how funny it sounds when I tell you how it all started and how I even consider it as a skillset. However, it wouldn't take long until you see how beneficial it could be for anyone.

After all, today, in order to be truly successful in leadership, politics, or any kind of negotiation, sales, business, and diplomacy, being able to learn how to analyze people would be truly beneficial. If you would like to find means to improve your career, it's important to learn how to read people's character and body language.

This book will teach you how to do this. By the end of this book, I hope you'll realize how easy it is to analyze a person by simply knowing where to look. By understanding what's really going on inside of them, you will see that influencing, persuading, and controlling them is fairly achievable.

You can do that by being able to know how to recognize a person's specific personality patterns and ways wherein they construct their internal experience.

For example, you are able to identify whether the person in front of you can take pressure well and can make himself calm during a stressful situation.

A great part of our lives will be spent getting on with others. We go on with our lives more efficiently if we can relate and connect well with people. And of course, life would be easier if we can easily know what goes inside the mind of the person in front of us and what kind of person they are in general.

In this book, you will learn an extremely practical system for rapidly determining the kind of person you are trying to deal with and how you are able to make the most out of your interaction. You'll discover how to connect with people in ways that they're going to respond to positively and just as significantly, how to evade useless misunderstandings.

This book, however, doesn't only focus on teaching you how to analyze other people, but also how you can analyze yourself to become aware of things you probably don't know about yourself as well as to celebrate your distinctive strengths.

This is also going to provide you with a pattern that will help you comprehend the different types of people you will get to encounter on a daily basis and how you can deal with them.

CHAPTER 1
ANALYZING YOURSELF

"Love yourself first before you love someone." This is a cliché we always hear when it comes to loving someone. This is true.

But to love someone, you need to know them. Not knowing yourself means not knowing your limits. This will heavily influence the level of your accomplishments as well as possibly aggravate your future plans.

A lot of people have wasted resources and efforts just because they didn't know what their limitations are. This is why analyzing yourself as well as your circumstances before doing something is vital.

The "self-analysis" must be all-embracing; it has to be done in every situation you will be in.

1.1 How to analyze yourself and understand what's going on in your own mind?

It's our human nature to constantly grow and change based on our personality and experiences. This is why it's imperative to take the time to perform self-analysis. This exercise will help you reflect on where you are in different aspects of your life. Together with this information, you can easily make essential adjustments and changes as you carry on and move forward in your life.

PART 1: EVALUATING YOUR SELF-ESTEEM

Step 1: Consider your childhood experiences. It's not always easy to understand who you are as a person and why you do things a certain way. Much more, what drives behavior and self-perception is our subconscious beliefs and attitudes. It is important to look deeper if you want to know how you really see yourself on a subliminal level. Here are important questions you must answer to know yourself better:

- ❖ Growing up, do you think you were listened to enough, or were you severely criticized?
- ❖ Were you spoken to with respect, or were you ignored or made fun of?
- ❖ Did you get enough affection and attention, or were you neglected?
- ❖ Were you abused physically, sexually, or verbally?
- ❖ Were you recognized for your accomplishments?
- ❖ Were your failures and shortcomings accepted or criticized?
- ❖ Were you pressured to be perfect?

By answering these questions, you will know where your attitudes or beliefs might be coming from. Walk down your memory lanes and relive your life as a child.

Step 2: Monitor your moods. For a whole day, carry a journal with you. Every time you feel a change in your mood, immediately write it down. This would be a way for you to identify your internal voice trying to communicate with you.

- ❖ The voice inside you isn't actually a voice whispering in your ears. Rather, it's the thoughts about your experiences. These thoughts are usually so deeply entrenched in the subconscious that you might not even realize you have them.
- ❖ The inner voice you would encounter might either be self-defeating or affirming. Individuals who have healthy self-esteem normally experience a positive, reassuring inner voice. On the other hand, those who have low self-esteem usually experience an inner voice that is punitive, castigatory, and critical.
- ❖ For some, documenting is not an easy task, especially if it triggers you to look back at the past traumas that you haven't fully moved on from. If journaling is something too upsetting for you or it gives you a hard time, you can turn to consult a counselor who is able to help you do this exercise easily.

Step 3: Note down your thoughts. The thoughts you're having immediately before your mood changes are a reflection of your inner voice. Known as the "automatic thoughts," they generally reflect how you perceive yourself and everything around you. Documenting these thoughts is going to help you see if a pattern emerges.

❖ Automatic thoughts come from the subconscious. That's why sometimes, pinpointing them can be quite challenging. For starters, you can ask yourself, "Why do I feel this way?" Then, you can also dig deeper by asking yourself further questions like "What does it have to do with who I am?" or "Why did I get affected like this?"

❖ Usually, the first answers you will get from yourself are pretty superficial ones. That's why you must keep asking, "What else?" until you can probe into your deeper automatic thoughts.

❖ For instance, if someone said something offensive, you can write something like, "I find what he said kind of annoying" "I felt angry when he said..." And after asking "What else?" several times, you might eventually identify a thought that you didn't think was there in the first place, like "I'm more impatient than I think I was."

Step 4: Assess your thought process. After writing down some automatic thoughts, you will start seeing a pattern. Figure out the underlying theme within your thoughts. Are your thoughts healthy and positive or are they self-defeating and negative? Common thought patterns that usually come from negative automatic thoughts include but are not limited to:

❖ All-or-none thinking takes place when you think that one mistake ruins everything. For example, when you make a mistake at your job, you might think that you're a total failure at your job.

❖ Debarring the positive is when you just focus on the bad things you did and completely forget about the positive or good thing you have done. For example, you may focus on the few answers that you got wrong on a test and complete ignore the fact that you've got most answers right.

❖ Jumping to conclusions is when you decide about the things without confirming their authenticity. For example, you might see your friend online on social media so you said hi. You saw him read your message but he didn't reply back right away. So, you automatically assume that he doesn't want to talk to you when in fact, he was just too busy doing something at the moment and was planning to reply back later.

❖ Labeling takes place when someone applies a label to himself or someone else instead of simply acknowledging the behavior or action. For example, rather than thinking, "I could have dealt with that better," you might think, "I am a horrible person."

Step 5: Check your self-esteem. Having healthy self-esteem may reflect your belief that you are worthwhile. Alternatively, if you have low self-esteem, you might feel poorly about yourself and constantly need the approval of other people. If you notice that you're having too many negative thoughts, then you might have low self-esteem. Having low self-esteem carries a negative effect on how you perceive yourself, so it's necessary to intentionally try to have a healthy and balanced perception of who you are as a person. If you are still uncertain whether you are experiencing low self-esteem, then you should become familiar with these three "faces" of negative self-esteem:

❖ **The Victim:** This is someone who acts like he is helpless and usually just sit and wait for someone to rescue him. He mastered the art of indifference or self-pity in order to conceal underlying fears of failing. He tends to be unassertive, might be an underachiever, and extremely reliant on other people for hope.

❖ **The Imposter:** This is someone who acts as if is happy and everything is going well when he is terrified of failure. The imposter has to always be successful to be happy, usually leading to competition, perfectionism, as well as stress.

❖ **The Rebel:** This is someone who constantly tries to downplay others, usually those who are of authority. The rebel tends to be angry all the time about not being good enough and tends to concentrate on not being hurt by the criticism of other people. This may lead to blaming others for his problems, and he may often oppose authority.

PART 2: UNDERSTANDING YOUR PERSONALITY TYPE

Get a piece of paper and place it in front of you. Make sure that the paper is in a vertical position. Place is on a hard surface so you can write on it easily.

On the paper, draw five lines vertically. These lines will create boxes which give you spaces to write, so see to it that there's enough space in between these lines.

In each space, write each following word: "Agreeableness," "Neuroticism," "Extraversion," "Conscientiousness," and "Openness to Experience." These words are the "The Big Five" personality traits. Based on many studies, these five personality traits show the general components of human personality that are most essential in interpersonal communications.

❖ Remember that these "Big Five" qualities aren't personality types but parts of the personality. For example, you might be high in "Agreeableness" or friendliness but pretty low with "Extraversion" or sociability. It's possible for someone to be very friendly but at the same time, not be very social.

❖ The "Emotional Stability" can also be referred to as the "Neuroticism" characteristic.

❖ In the same way, "Openness to Experience" can sometimes be referred to as "Intellect."

Figure out where you are on all the five dimensions. It's common for people to mostly fall in the high spectrum or the low spectrum of every personality dimension. Take some time to consider where you really belong. Put "High" or "Low" in every corresponding box that you made. Below are descriptions of every trait in order to guide you with your self-assessment:

❖ Extroversion is a reflection of a keen interest in other people as well as external events. People that are very extroverted tend to have more confidence and don't have any problem exploring unexplored territories. On the other hand, those who are low in extroversion are usually referred to as "introverts" and tend to isolate themselves and enjoy quiet environments.

❖ Neuroticism refers to the anxiety level. Those who are high in this dimension generally experience negative emotions, which are usually stronger compared to their counterparts. If you're always worrying and always seem to be freaking out, then you're probably high in this area.

❖ Openness to Experience specifies how willing you are to adjust your thinking when something new arises. A person who is high in this area is someone who is probably eccentric and free-spirited. If you happen to be low in this area, then chances are, you are more conventional and tangible with your thinking patterns.

❖ Conscientiousness is how much you consider other people every time you need to make a decision. This also reflects your level of self-control. If you happen to be high in this area, then you're probably well-organized, efficient, and function properly with independence. If you happen to be low in this area, then you might be spontaneous and impulsive and do well in places and situations that are always changing.

❖ Agreeableness specifies the level to which someone is compatible with other people. This also shows how much someone cares about other people. If you happen to be high in this area, then chances are, you're pretty empathetic and it's so easy for you to relate to and understand others. People might describe you as "nice" and "kind-hearted." On the other hand, if you are low in this area, then you don't put a lot of emphasis on your and other people's emotions when making any form of actions.

Ponder how these traits affect your personality. It's human nature for us to exhibit behavior and choose environments depending on what we feel is comfortable for our personality. This self-assessment exercise might provide you with a great understanding of why you act or think a certain way.

PART 3: WRITING A SELF-ASSESSMENT FOR WORK

Pick the right time. Make sure to save some time for this exercise as this quick self-reflection can be really beneficial for you. During this time, you will want to concentrate on your goals, habits, competencies, as well as overall performance. Simply spending an hour to review personal notes and other details is going to help you write a precise self-evaluation of how you do see yourself.

Write down your accomplishments from your workplace throughout the past year. You don't have to be shy about writing all the things you achieved – you worked hard for them. There's nothing wrong about being proud of yourself. The main purpose of self-analysis is to highlight all of your accomplishments. Think of all of the projects that you have done, extra responsibilities that you performed, and all the hard work you did just to benefit the company you are working for. When it's possible, use these specific examples throughout your self-assessment.

❖ You can check back on your previous emails in order for you to remember some of your accomplishments that you might have already forgotten.

❖ If you have a folder on your computer where you save all your previous assignments, check it out to see if you have documents that will remind you of your previous achievements.

Document the areas that you'd want to improve on. It's so tempting to only focus on your accomplishments. However, pinpointing the areas you need improvements in is very important when it comes to self-analysis. Consider areas you wish you were better in to attain your goals more efficiently. When you reflect your challenges as well, you are able to get a more precise reflection of your actual performance.

Make a list of goals that you'd want to accomplish in the following year. This would be your action plan, and you must concentrate on things that you are able to do to improve your performance at work. See to it that the goals evidently show your commitment to giving more value to your workplace.

PART 4: MEASURING YOUR LEVEL OF STRESS

Recall any life changes that happened to you recently. Good changes and bad changes happen and become normal in an adult's life. Some of the good changes include getting a higher paying job, moving to a new house, getting a promotion, or getting married, while the bad ones include being laid off, losing someone close to you, breakup, etc. You have to remember that any kind of change can be pretty stressful as you will need to make some sort of adjustment. Take your time to consider and list down all the changes that you might have experienced in the last few months that might have caused you stress and pain.

Dwell on your values. When you live a life that contradicts with your values and beliefs, then expect to experience a high level of stress. For instance, if you're someone who is very ambitious and competitive, but you are stuck in a dull dead-end job, then this life that is not aligned will also cause you a great amount of stress. If your values and belief systems don't match your actual life experience, you might have a life that is filled with stress and discontentment. Here are important questions you should ask yourself in order to identify if there are any mismatches in your life that causes you stress:

- ❖ What values in life do you give importance to? Success? Family? Hobbies? Kindness? Religious beliefs?

- ❖ Do your actions and lifestyle conflict with these values? For example, say one of your values is making your family happy. Do you really spend enough time with them to make them happy?

- ❖ Do your hobbies, job, relationships, or other aspects of your life conflict with these values?

See the things around you. The places you go and the things you do – how much do they contribute to the stress levels you have to deal with? If you are living in a place that is surrounded by crime, pollution, trash, or any other unpleasant elements, then you are also likely dealing with stress a lot. Figure out the source of stress.

Think about your personal issues and social dynamics. Personal issues and social factors can have a great effect on your stress level. Below are some aspects to consider when you're trying to assess how these features are affecting your stress level:

- ❖ Finances: Do you have enough funds to afford your basic and daily needs?

- ❖ Family: Is everyone in the family alright and in a good situation?

- ❖ Health: Is your health and that of your family in a good condition?

Monitor your sleep. Not getting enough sleep can highly affect a lot of areas of your life, which of course can boost the levels of your stress. Track the length of your sleep every night. Even though the amount of sleep that one needs varies from person to person, the average duration of sleep should be 6 to 8 hours and many adults have a hard time attaining those numbers. Because of this, your stress levels might be higher compared to people who get enough sleep. Here are the areas of your life that can be affected by lack of sleep:

- ❖ Your thinking process
- ❖ Difficulty in focusing
- ❖ Health problems, including a high risk of chronic diseases
- ❖ Forgetfulness
- ❖ Lower libido
- ❖ Early aging
- ❖ Weight gain

Think of the ways how you can manage your stress. List down all the things that you are able to do in order to improve your life. After all, the main objective of self-analysis is to promote growth in your life.

How does this help you analyze others?

Being able to understand yourself better can also help you improve your capacity to better understand other people's thoughts and emotions.

A German study suggests that those who participated in a psychology-training program to improve their "perspective-taking", which is a term used by psychologists to describe the ability to know the "inner world" of another person became better at analyzing themselves and analyzing others. The term inner world means a person's beliefs, thoughts, emotions, and personality.

One study published in the Journal of Cognitive Enhancement shows there's some truth to the saying that, "In order to know someone, you must know yourself first."

Knowing yourself completely at a deeper level isn't simply just to boost your ego. When you know yourself better, it's going to be easier for you to view yourself from another person's perspective. It is also going to be useful in improving your social skills.

Looking Inward

There was a study where researchers looked into data gathered from two groups of approximately 80 adults each who were all living in Germany and were between the ages of 20 and 55.

The study consisted of a 3-day retreat followed by a 2-hour meeting every week throughout the following 3 months. The people who participated were trained to develop skills to help them improve their inner awareness. Some of the skills they tried to develop were how to keep doing meditation exercise regularly wherein they observed the thoughts that came up into their heads without being emotionally involved.

This exercise was designed to help the participants get more understanding of how their minds work without reacting too much to it.

Some other skills that were assigned involved improving their "inner parts" that were related to their own psyche, such as optimism, judgment, management, etc.

The participants were asked to observe the "inner parts" that would be stimulated within themselves in daily situations, like every time they are at work, when they are playing with their kids, or other things that you usually do within the day.

Throughout one session, the participants worked in pairs in order to complete an exercise wherein one of them acted as a speaker and chose a recent situation that happened to him but described it from the standpoint of one of their inner parts. Throughout the exercise, a participant listened and tried to guess the speaker's inner parts that the speaker was trying to portray. This is an activity that improves perspective-taking or understanding the thoughts of other people.

By performing this exercise on a regular basis, one can detach from the inner parts that are routinely stimulated in certain circumstances. This lets them be more flexible when it comes to their typical behavior patterns.

Understanding others

Based on the study, the more participants recognized these internal characteristics of personality, the better they understood other people's intentions and beliefs.

Fascinatingly, the research found that those who could recognize more negative inner parts of personality were more likely to have improvements in analyzing others. It was kind of astounding that being able to recognize positive inner parts wasn't associated with a better analysis of other people. It looks like that in most participants, being able to recognize the negative inner parts was what really improved skills and dedication.

In order to face your own negative inner parts, you might have to go through your inner resistance against some painful emotions, so maybe that is the reason why people who faced these parts had a better understanding of other people.

Even though not everyone might have access to the form of training used in this research, there are many other ways to acquire similar skills and understanding.

Mindfulness training, meditation, and other forms of self-inquiry could all be great experiences.

1.2 How to Understand Your Thoughts, Behaviors, and Actions

According to Science, our thoughts on everything that happens to us can have a huge effect on the way we feel. I'm not only talking about the big things that happen to us but even the smallest issues. However, our thinking is not always accurate or obvious. If you become more familiar with our thinking patterns, you will have more understanding with others.

It's so easy to believe that every time something bad happen to us, we use it as our foundation for what we feel and our decisions. However, studies have shown that it's not really the event itself that triggers our emotional reaction. Instead, it is the automatic thoughts that go through our head in instant response to the event. However, our emotional reaction could be so fast that our thoughts are not very obvious.

While our thoughts and emotional responses will be appropriate in most occasions, there might still be times that they will not. If you happen to have inappropriate thoughts, especially in reaction to negative events, they are able to drive stronger reactions and emotions than needed. Furthermore, we can fall into patterns that could be harmful to our happiness not only temporarily but also in the longer term.

There have been proofs that suggest that if we can become good at recognizing our thoughts when it comes to things that happen and when these are not accurate, we can become better at analyzing and managing our emotional reactions.

This might have a great effect on our own happiness and also on our interactions with the people we work or live with.

Getting Started

1. Breaking things down into ABC

The first thing you have to do is to learn how you can unravel your feelings, thoughts, and actions.

One of the founders of cognitive behavioral therapy, Dr. Albert Ellis, developed what's usually known the A-B-C model that is a great way to separate things out.

The letter **A** stands for **A**ctivating Event, which refers to the things that have taken place; B stands for **B**elief, which are the thoughts that directly come up in our head; and **C** is for **C**onsequences, which are the emotions we have and how we are reacting consequently.

Dr. Ellis found that the way people interpret things that are taking place in their lives and the things they say to themselves (B) play a big part in how they feel emotionally and how they behave (C).

Below are examples that show how people thinking differently about the same event can affect people's feelings and behaviors differently.

Example #1: **A**ctivating event

You're grinding hard for an upcoming deadline. Your boss asks you multiple times that week about the report and reminds you that he wants to see it first before it goes to the client.

Person 1:

Belief - "My boss doesn't trust me and that I'm incapable of doing this by myself. He thinks that I'm just messing around not doing it."

Consequences — He feels worried, pressured, and stressed. He has a hard time concentrating on the report and makes mistakes. He has trouble sleeping.

Person 2:

Belief - "YES! This project is very important and thankfully, my boss keeps checking in and that he wants to read it to make sure that it will be okay with the client."

Consequences - He feels calmed and supported. He continues working on the report, excited to show the result to the boss.

Example 2: **A**ctivating event

You're having a bad day. Walking home, you saw your friend a few meters away walking toward the other direction. You wave at him and it seems like he just ignored you.

Person 1:

Belief - "I can't believe he just ignored me. I might have done something that made him upset. Or perhaps, he just doesn't want to talk to me at all."

Consequences - He feels upset and down, not bothering to call or text his friend anymore. He stays inside and prefers not to talk with anyone.

Person2:

Belief – "He looked so distracted, and he didn't even notice me. I hope he's fine."

Consequences - He feels alright, pretty worried about the friend. He calls his friend to see if he's okay.

So, which one are you, the Person 1 or the Person 2?

2. Challenging your thoughts

For most of us, tuning into our thoughts or beliefs is something that is not easy. Most of the time, an event is going to activate some sort of emotional response in us that is going to affect our behavior. Usually, unless we take a minute and do some reflection, we are either unconscious of our thoughts with regard to the event that generated the emotion, or we leave our interpretation unopposed.

Of course, it might be that our interpretations are right and the way we feel and act in response is suitable. But by tuning into the things, we tell ourselves to think more thoroughly and carefully. We let ourselves be challenged by those thoughts that are illogical or harmful by asking ourselves questions like:

- ❖ What proofs do we have that says our thoughts are true?
- ❖ What could be the other reasons why this happened?

- ❖ Is thinking the way I currently do would help the situation?
- ❖ If my thoughts are correct, what can I do to fix the issue?

By asking yourself the logical questions, you can prevent yourself from getting into bad or negative places. It allows you to hold the fort of how you choose to react.

In Example 2 mentioned above, the Person 1 could have challenged himself by asking what proof he has that he has done something bad that upset his friend – maybe the friend was rushing to do something to even notice you or that he was not wearing his eyeglasses. If he thinks these thoughts, then he could save himself from feeling down and becoming worried.

When something makes you feel upset or worried, or when anything gives you negative feelings, try this ABC exercise on yourself. And if you make it a habit, you will see how it can make your life happier and less stressful.

3. Finding the patterns

By becoming adapted at tuning in to the way you look at things and interpret events, you may begin to notice that you say the same things to yourself time and again.

Maybe, you're someone who constantly blames himself or constantly blames other people when things go bad or someone who believes they're not doing good enough and other people are better than them. Maybe you're prone to worrying about things all the time – even though those things may not, and often don't, happen.

As you can see in the ABC example mentioned above, every means of interpreting an event has an effect on our actions and emotions. If we develop a specific obstructive pattern of thoughts, it's possible that certain emotions will also become accustomed to us. For instance, people who blame themselves are more likely to experience feelings of guilt or sadness, while those who tend to blame other people will feel angrier. Those who feel they are not good enough are likely to feel sad or shameful.

1.3 Understanding Other People's Traits and Flaws

It's generally a good idea to hold yourself to high standards and go all-out. But there are times when people have unrealistic beliefs when it comes to things that they are capable of and should do. The standards they set are impractically high. Then if they make a mistake, they might get too disappointed and unforgiving to themselves. That is a bad form of *perfectionism*. This is when someone sees as unacceptable anything but being perfect. These feelings can increase stress and bring about signs of depression.

However, self-compassion could help you protect yourself from such negative impacts. Self-compassion can be described as treating yourself how you would describe your best friend.

When things go wrong, it's so easy to say good things to other people to console them. However, it's even easier to choose to be mean to yourself. But even if it's the case, many of us still can't still understand people.

A lot of us complain about others, usually about people who do the same thing over and over again. I must admit, I used to be that person who complains a lot about others. Some of the things you would hear from me included:

- ❖ He's so annoying.
- ❖ I hate it when people are always late; why can't they respect other people's time?!
- ❖ I would never do that to anyone. He's such a horrible person for even thinking about that!
- ❖ Our neighbors are always fighting;, sometimes it keeps me up all night because I can hear them arguing.
- ❖ It's so disgusting how some people would leave dirty dishes and not wash them right away.

But now, I came to a realization that I don't have to like other people and they don't have to change because of me. All I can do is to accept them with their flaws and who they are as a person.

It's all up to me how I am going to deal with them. I mean, I can criticize them all day long, but at the end of the day, it's their life and they are the only ones to deal with it.

This is what I call Reality Training, which is recognizing that if you don't have a happier life, then you must learn how to accept people as they are and look for ways how you can deal with them, or just completely get them out of the picture.

It's all up to you whether or not you want to tolerate them or simply walk away from them because of their traits that you don't like. *That's the reality of it!* The truth is, you will only have two options; it's either you stop dealing with the person completely, or accept that person and adjust to how they are. Trying to change the person is not the best option because first of all, it's not always effective, and secondly, imagine someone trying to change you... would you like it? Voluntarily changing how you react to that person's flaws would be one of the best choices.

Not everyone will change just because you said so. That's why if you want to fix the situation, you're the one who needs to control your reaction. When I recognized this, I was still in the early phase of my marriage. It really drove me insane whenever my wife would tell me that she wants to watch a movie with me in bed. She would fall asleep within the next 15 minutes in the movie – I complained about it whenever she did it.

She kept telling me that she was just tired but she didn't mean to piss me off or anything. I then realized that she's right; she meant well. So, every time she asks for movies, I just let her sleep. I still finished the movies and even turned the volume low so she could sleep better. I accepted this thing about her that I initially thought was annoying, and I'm sure she did accept the things about me that she might have found annoying as well – I'm not perfect. I try to consider things and accept things about her to avoid pointless arguments and to make her happy and it worked; many things that I found annoying no longer affect me.

Adjust your expectations.

What you might think wrong might not look wrong to others. If you feel like something is unacceptable, handle it in a different way. Being self-righteous over something that you disagree with triggers needless stress. Giving someone sermons about good behavior usually does nothing.

Once I learned this reality, I told my colleague who used to annoy me all the time by being late, "Meet me at this restaurant. I will already order my appetizer, so I can eat while waiting." Then I have a friend who would bail out the last minute before the meet up we agreed. So, I did the same thing once. He got a little frustrated. I told him I just couldn't take him seriously because he always cancelled the last minute. He apologized and said he would not do it again, and to this day, he always kept his promise. All because I decided to change how I respond to the situations! Sometimes, people give better response to actions than complaints.

Here are some circumstances that portray common realities:

Reality: *Parents usually see things differently because they stick to older values.*

Having an argument with parents can be really frustrating. Because they grew up with different values, they are not as open-minded as today's generation. For many of them, if they don't understand what you are doing, then you're probably wrong. Instead of arguing with them, it's better to work with that reality. Accept the fact that no matter how much you explain things to them, they'll never get them. Forcing them to understand things would be unnecessary. You don't have to bother. And because your parents wouldn't change their thoughts about it, you can simply change your ways instead. You can tell them that they might not understand you, but it's okay. Assure them that nothing's wrong with what you are doing or thinking and there's no point arguing about it.

Reality: *We might have friends that have annoying traits.*

If you are friends with someone you like hanging out with but they are always late, instead of being annoyed that they are always late, you can change your response. It is your choice to be friends and make a plan with someone who you know might keep you waiting all the time. If you know he's always late, then why don't you arrive late or set the time of the meeting earlier?

If you have a friend who talks a lot, try to accept that it's a part of his personality. After all, it's better to have a talkative friend than having someone next to you who just nods and say nothing.

If your friend would always invite to see you but bail out the last minute, then the next time he calls to see you, tell him you're the one who would call and tell him when you're not busy anymore.

If you have a friend who would borrow money and would not pay you within the promised timeframe, then you must remind yourself that it was never your obligation to lend him money, so next time he asks, refuse.

If you raised the issue to someone but they still kept doing what they were doing, then it's time to give up. You have to do what you have to do. If their behavior bothers you, avoid the situation to get to that point. You know what they say, prevention is better than cure!

CHAPTER 2
ANALYZING OTHERS

First of all, before analyzing someone, there's one question you need to answer…

"Why do I need to analyze this person?"

You need to perform analysis about another person normally tells you the type of analysis that has to be performed. If someone's applying for a job, then a certain type of analysis is used. On the other hand, if you are performing analysis on someone for mental disturbance, then another set of procedures has to be used.

Once you have answered the question as to why you must do it, then you can then proceed. Now, let's assume that you are evaluating someone for a job application.

Then the next question you have to figure out the answer to is, what are the strengths of the person? However, of course, the right answer will usually depend on the strengths that are necessary for the position. In this as well, we usually have to follow the needs of the assessment. If you think that leadership skills would be necessary, then you may want to focus on finding "sociability" and "dominant" traits.

After learning the applicant's strengths, the next thing you need to be aware of is his weaknesses. You have to know the traits that may affect the person's performance negatively. Can they be considered as impulsive, easily distracted, or easily pressured?

Having a general list is useful since it usually highlights problems and traits that weren't initially considered. In this sense, your analysis normally starts with a screening for the most common general traits and a screening for psychopathology.

2.1 What Does Analyzing Someone Involve?

While it's impossible to read someone's innermost feelings and thoughts, there is still another way to read someone, and that is through his body language. On top of that, a person's eyes are usually very communicative as well.

This reminds me of the time I met this guy called Dan at the gym. I mean, we never really had an actual conversation, but I noticed how he came at the gym every day at the same time. I know this sounds like a pretty insignificant detail for a lot of people, but for someone who knows how to analyze people, this detail meant a lot.

Dan was self-motivated, determined, organized, and very consistent with his goals. These traits became obvious to me only because I noticed how punctual he was.

But aside from that, there are other things that I noticed about this guy. He would wear tank tops that showed his muscular physique, and he would do exercises that are not normally done by most people in the gym. This made me think that he's a guy who loved showing up. When doing further analysis, I figured out that he's an only child in the family.

When you are analyzing someone's personality, you have to keep in mind that the person's birth order plays a part in his personality. Most of the time, children that have no siblings are showered with attention growing up and that is the reason why even when they grow old, they still crave for attention.

The guy loved wearing black; he would wear black all the time, even after his work out – especially after work out, actually. When he took out his phone from his pocket, its cover was also black. Even the car he drove was black.

When analyzing the personality of someone, you should understand that people may go too extreme when they want to escape from something. Coming to the gym regularly and wearing black showed that the guy wanted to look tough and strong.

When I gathered further information, I learned that my assumptions were true. When the guy was still a little kid, he used to be bullied at school, and he felt like he was a weak person. That's why when he grew up, he promised to not appear weak. He started going to the gym regularly and wore black all the time to cover and run away from his past.

Another aspect you have to consider when analyzing the personality of a person is that connecting the dots must always initiate with a straight line. So, what does it mean? Well, it means that if my speculations were true, then definitely, we must expect to find that he's doing other activities that were able to help him become stronger apart from coming to the gym.

And my guess was true; Dan was also doing martial arts.

Here are some tips for you to get started:

Be Objective

You must to go at it without prejudice or being biased. There's undeniably no point in "objectively" doing your best analyzing someone if you've already had a stereotype for them. You have to get rid of all the layers of prejudice in order for you to see beyond your first impression.

Look at Non-verbal Signs

Your approach to analyzing someone must be a combination of being steered by your intuition, emotional intelligence, as well as observing the person's behavior and physical movements.

Most of the time, people would lean their body in the direction of something they like and lean away from something that makes them angry or uncomfortable. The same thing goes for which directions the person's toes are pointed. If they're pointing their body and feet right at you, it's possibly a sign that they're comfortable with you or want to talk to you.

Is someone biting his nails? This could be an indication that the person might be feeling anxious or nervous. This is something that is extremely common for people who are under pressure.

Other signs of someone feeling tension might be seen in facial expressions. Grinding of teeth, gritting of teeth, and puckered lips might show that they're feeling upset and are trying to inhibit what they're wanting to say.

What's the posture telling you?

It's not difficult to notice confidence in a person by simply looking at how someone carries himself. If you see them cowering or slouching, it might be a sign that they might have low self-esteem. You will see a clear line between a posture that radiates confidence and the exaggerated swagger that goes with an inflated ego.

Create a baseline

Most of us carry some sort of behavioral quirks. Sometimes, these behavior patterns are habitual. Some of these quirks include scratching of head, clearing their throat before they talk, looking at the floor, and fondling the back of their necks. You have to read what the "normal" behavior of the person is. That's going to be your baseline. It's not a good thing to overanalyze that someone is feeling nervous or telling a lie only because you saw them biting their fingernails. Nail biting is a known mannerism for many, so it could be something normal. So, make sure to take that in consideration.

Look for Clusters

The moment you've established a baseline for the person you're talking to, search for clusters of behavior that are not included in the baseline. Did you notice any sort of contradiction between their physical gestures and their normal behavior?

Another thing that can help you point out a baseline inconsistency is Phoneme awareness. This is a basic component of phonetic speech. If a person is feeling extremely nervous or is lying, you might notice how their voice might raise or lower. They may overstress certain words as overcompensation in order to manipulate you to make you believe them.

It doesn't mean that because someone has a very loud voice, he's the strongest person in the room. Although people with loud, big voice might be intimidating, having a loud voice might just indicate someone's confidence. Unless of course if you're dealing with someone who manipulates with a personality issue. Sociopaths or psychopaths are usually hard to read since people cannot see past their charm.

Consider Context

While it's true that crossed arms might be an indication that someone's closing himself off because he might not feel comfortable in the situation he is in, but it's also possible that he's just feeling cold. It's important to be observant in order to broaden your field of focus and also not to get preoccupied with one tell-tale sign.

Understand Your Intuition

It's important to trust your gut. It's important that you open yourself up to their vibe and try to make sense of the emotions and feelings a person induces in you. Natural instinct plays a big part in our daily life, so it's very important. This is not about trying to read someone's aura. It's about reading how one's body and mind work to their presence every time they have an encounter.

Bottom Line

Analyzing people isn't just about protecting ourselves from prospective liars and scammers. The main goal for learning how to analyze someone isn't to train yourself to be a criminal profiler. The goal of this is to improve your observation skills in order for you to make better decisions in your life. Being able to analyze people we're working with or interacting with can help a great deal in our lives.

Why learn to do this? What are the benefits?

Why do you think that we tend to get along so well with some people while there are some people that we just can't manage to be with? Why is that there are times it's so easy to predict how someone will react to a certain situation? Well, there's a big chance that it has to do with that person's personality type preference.

The truth is, each of us has a specific preference that makes up our type of personality and it just happens that some personalities work better together than others.

Chances are, your personality might work so well with one person and might not work so well with another.

A person's type of personality, together with his opinions, work ethics, as well as attitude, plays a part in making it easy or hard to get along with others. However, when you are aware of your own personality, it's going to be easier for you to observe and adapt to other people and even the situation around you. With this awareness, you will be able to learn not only about yourself but also about others.

The Myers-Briggs Personality Type Indicator, which we will talk about further later in this book, gives a great detailed analysis into the main personality preferences and leanings a person has – it goes deeper on the differences between thinking and feeling, introversion and extraversion, intuition and sensing, etc.

But then again, this kind of assessment is not necessary to be able to truly understand yourself and other people around you. By becoming more self-aware and having acceptance for those people around you, no matter how different they are from you, you will be able to reap these benefits:

You will be aware of your preferences. Each person has their own psychological type inclinations and working within these inclinations usually lets us be most effective, efficient, and our most comfortable with ourselves. On the other hand, working beyond these limits will require you more time and energy and normally leads to lower quality work. Being aware of these boundaries — and knowing when you are within or beyond them —helps you improve your efficiency, productivity, and time management skills.

You can avoid conflict. By being mindful of other people's personality, you can prevent conflicts. If you know how other people may have a tendency to be impulsive whenever something comes up, it becomes easier for you to adjust your reaction.

You can appreciate diversity. Recognizing how your personality type differs from and interacts with other types can provide you with a great appreciation for people's differences and what it offers to your life. Sometimes, it is just really nice to have that very creative mind that helps you create ideas that only certain minds can come up with.

You can choose the right people. A big part of being an adult is the necessity to choose which ones to keep and which ones to avoid. As adults, we want to get rid of those who bring toxic vibes in our lives and make it more difficult than it already is. And the first step to know which ones you need in your life is to learn about their personalities.

The concept behind personality type is that it's something we are born with, live with, as well as die with. It is something that develops and evolves over time. It is up to us how we use it or apply it differently based on our experiences. However, it is something that normally stays the same our whole life. By entirely understanding personality types of each person you interact with, you are able to learn to appreciate their strong points and also recognize and accept their weaknesses. On top of it, you also learn your capacity to accept people for who they are.

2.2 How to analyze someone using effective techniques

As a psychiatrist, it is part of my job to read people, not only based on what they say but also who they are as a person. It is my job to interpret their verbal and nonverbal cues to learn what kind of people they are. Logic alone is not enough to learn a person's whole story. It is necessary to surrender other vital kinds of information in order to learn how to read the necessary non-verbal instinctive cues that people radiate. In order to do this, you should also be willing to submit to any biases or emotional baggage like old hatreds or ego clashes that holds you back from seeing someone's personality and characters clearly. The key is to stay objective and get information impartially without misrepresenting it.

Whether you are trying to read your friend, co-worker, or partner in order to understand them exactly, it's important to surrender biases, and all kinds of walls should be destroyed. You need to be ready to get rid of old, restrictive ideas you might have. Those people who can read other people well are skilled to read the invisible. They have learned to use what I like to call the "super-senses" to look beyond where you normally put your attention in order to access life-changing instinctive visions.

Three Techniques to Analyze People

1. Reading the Body Language

Studies have shown that words account for just 7% of how people communicate while our body language gives off 55% and the tone of our voice tone about 30%. Here, a vital point to keep in mind is that you are not trying too hard to read someone's body language. It wouldn't help to be too analytical. Just stay relaxed and adaptable. Stay comfortable, relax, and just observe.

> Observe the Appearance

Before fully reading a person's body language, here is something you might want to notice first: What do they wear? Are they wearing refined, suited up clothing or are they just wearing relaxed jeans and shirt preferring to look and feel all casual? Are they wearing revealing clothing that show up too much skin? Or perhaps they are wearing accessories that represent their spiritual or religious beliefs? Most of the time, how a person represents himself based on his clothing says a lot about his personality.

> Look at the Body Posture

Here is something you must ask yourself when reading someone's body posture: Do they always hold their heads high looking all confident? Or do you notice them walk irresolutely or shy away, which can be a sign of having low self-esteem? Do they carry themselves with a chest all puffed out, which can be a sign of having a huge ego?

> Notice the Physical Movements

- ❖ *Leaning and distance* – Check out where they lean. Normally, we lean toward the things that we like and try to stay away from the ones we don't.
- ❖ *Crossed legs and arms* – These poses may suggest being angry, defensive, or protective. When you see someone crossing their legs, they tend to point their foot toward someone they feel comfortable with.
- ❖ *Hiding of hands* – When you see someone put their hands in their pockets, laps, or just anywhere they can't be seen, it may suggest that they are not very comfortable.
- ❖ *Cuticle picking or biting of lips* – When you notice someone biting or licking their lips or picking their cuticles, it might be their way of soothing themselves under a situation that makes them feel awkward or pressurized.

> Understand Facial Expressions

Feelings can become imprinted on our facial expressions, and this is definitely the easiest thing to learn how to read. When you see someone's face with deep frown lines, that may suggest overthinking or feeling worried. On the other hand, crow's feet indicate smile lines of joy. When you see someone with pursed lips, it is probably a sign of anger, bitterness, or contempt. You'll know someone is angry when you notice him with a clenched jaw and grinding teeth.

2. Listen to Your Intuition

You are able to tune into someone further than their words and body language. Intuition is what you feel in your guts and not what you hear your head say. It is the nonverbal details that you see through pictures and ah-has, instead of logic. If you would like to truly get to understand someone, the most important thing you must understand is who the person is from the inside, and not who they seem like from the outside. Intuition allows you to see beyond the obvious to tell you more about the story.

Intuitive Cues Checklist

✓ *Acknowledge your gut feelings*

Feel your guts and honor it, especially the first time you meet someone; it's an intuitive reaction that takes place before having a chance to think. It conveys whether you feel comfortable or not. Gut feelings take place in an instant – it's a primal, immediate response. They are your inner truth pattern, which relays if you are able to trust people.

✓ *Don't ignore the goosebumps*

Goosebumps are spectacular intuitive stings that say that we resound with people who affect us or are saying something that moves us. We also get goosebumps whenever we experience Deja-vu, which is a recognition that we experience during the time we feel like we've already known or experienced something.

✓ *Heed the flashes of insight*

During normal conversations, you might get an "ah-ha" about those who come out of the blue. Be alert. Otherwise, you'll probably be going to miss it. Sometimes, we just tend to go onto the next thought so quickly that we lose critical insights immediately.

✓ *Be aware of intuitive empathy*

Sometimes you are able to feel emotions in your body and even physical symptoms of other people which can be considered as a strong form of empathy. So, when you're trying to analyze someone, try to notice: "Do I feel down when I was talking to him? Does it make me feel heavy when I'm around him?"

3. Sense the Emotional Energy

Human emotions are a great expression of our energy; this is what we like to call the "vibe". We use it together with intuition. There are some people who we feel good to be around; you know, those people who can easily improve our vitality and mood. On the other hand, there are people who are just so draining; the ones we immediately want to avoid as soon as we feel their presence. This is a "subtle energy" that we can feel inches or feet away from the body even if we don't feel them visually. In Chinese medicine, this is what they called the *chi,* an essential vitality that plays a part in a human's overall wellbeing.

Strategies to Read Emotional Energy

1. Sense the presence of others

This is the energy that we are emitting, not essentially corresponding with our behavior or words. It is the emotional atmosphere that goes around us such as a drizzled rain and ray of sunshine. When trying to read or analyze someone, ask this question: Do you feel a friendly presence around them? Or seeing them makes you want to avoid them?

2. Look them in the eyes

Our eyes are the most expressive part of the body, and they are good at transmitting powerful energy. Just like how our brain has an electromagnetic sign that extends beyond the body, research shows that our eyes can project this as well. As much as possible, you want to take time observing people's eyes. Are they lazy? Reclusive? Outgoing? Approachable? Bored? Angry?

3. Notice the way they interact

As humans, we like sharing emotional energy with physical contact, and it goes throughout like an electrical current. Whenever you make interactions like hugging, handshaking, or even by simply tapping, ask yourself, does it make you feel warm? Do the way they do it feels confident or comfortable? Or does it put you off? Is the person's hand shaky, which indicates nervousness or anxiety? Or does it feel like they are simply forced to do those interactions?

4. Listen for the tone of their reaction

The way someone talks – through tone and volume – can tell so much about a person's emotions. The frequencies of the sound generate vibrations. When you read people, notice how the tone of their voice makes you feel. Ask yourself: Does it feel soothing? Snippy? Sarcastic? Abrasive?

2.3 How to Tell If Someone Has A Bad Character or Good Character

In order to best identify if someone has a bad or good character, you must answer this question clearly first: What do you consider a good and a bad character?

There are a lot of different opinions when it comes to what's good and bad traits. There are a lot of popular traits that most of us consider good or bad, but all in all, it's subjective and it all depends on you.

Even though you'd know the most common traits, you'd still be averaging those characteristics and again, you'd need to choose which of the many possibilities you agree on.

Take your time to list down all the pros and cons of having different character traits. From the list you make, write the ones you think are good and bad. Now, when analyzing someone, find what traits they have that belong to the good and bad lists you made. However, you must keep in mind that to know a person's traits, you might need to get to know them a little longer than just basing it on the first impression. Otherwise, your chance of being wrong is high.

The more we spend time to get to know someone, the more we understand why they act a certain way and the more it becomes easy for us to accept them. Once you start to accept someone for the traits they have, you might start seeing those traits as not bad ones.

Overall, a good or bad character is still based on what you think it is. When it comes to what others think of you, asking them is the best way to find out. And yes, while finding out the difference between good and bad traits can be a long process, it is worth the energy and time you put in.

If you want a shortcut, then follow your instinct and don't judge people. You just use your instinct to guide you on who to avoid and who to keep around. Judging is biased and not at all reliable. When it comes to fully getting to know a person, it's almost impossible to do that no matter how long you've known that person; it is only that person who knows who he truly is.

Analyzing Someone Based on How He Treats Others

The most important relationship you will have in your life is the relationship you will have with yourself. This is not to say that other relationships shouldn't matter that much. However, at the end of the day, no one cares about you more than you do.

Every person wants to be liked and accepted by others. Fitting in with others is human nature. When you act instinctively without being thinking about your intentions, you're performing unconscious commands.

This is why it's easy to read someone's personality based on how they treat others.

If someone treats people or you badly by being either rude, uncompassionate, insensitive, disrespectful, violent, they are extremely unreliable or untrustworthy; They might tell many lies or just spread gossips; you would want to steer clear of those people in your life. You are able to judge for yourself based on the way a person behaves towards other people. Allow your instincts to do the job of deciding things for you. They're already judging others, and there's a big possibility that they are also judging you. Admit it, there were probably times when you quietly judged people who you know judge others or treat other people like crap. They treat most people badly, there is then a recurring pattern developing. If I see someone treat others badly, I keep myself aware of it and I try not to deal with them at all costs.

On the other hand, when someone is nice to other people, it's so easy to assume that they are great people. We love to be around them, and in return, it's so easy to be nice to them. After all, the saying that "treat others the way they treat you" is so easy to follow. But what if they only do that to look good because they have negative intentions? Perhaps they use this attitude to mask their real personality.

But then again, this is only one way to analyze someone. It's still important to take information from multiple different perspectives and use your logic by considering possible scenarios as to why a person would respond or act this way and saving actual judgment until you're extremely sure rather than simply passing judgment irrationally and without cause.

For example, maybe someone is mean to another person because that person did something awful to him, but the reality is that he is the nicest person you'd ever meet. Similarly, someone might initially show up as the nicest person but when we're not looking, they are just simply horrible.

All in all, even though analyzing someone based on how they treat people is effective most of the time, other times, that's not who they are, and there's a deeper reason as to why they act a certain way toward others. It would be a great idea to observe and consider other possibilities instead of committing to a certain action or thought inconsiderately or foolishly.

2.4 How to Analyze Someone Through Their Environment

Identifying confidence & insecurity

- **How to differentiate**

In the society we have today, it seems like confidence is usually seen as a sign of being independent, strong, and even being smart. On the contrary of that is insecurity, which might have seen as being timid, shy, and even anti-social. Insecurity manifests itself in a person by holding them back in life due to fear. This is where the battle of insecurity against confidence starts.

Yes, these usually are the first impressions on these two different personalities. However, it's always beyond that. Actually, the entire picture will look different based on your unique situation. Each person has their own strengths, weaknesses, challenges, and achievements. We tend to feel confident and insecure in certain situations.

We can only hope for confidence to rule our lives rather than our insecurities. One of the best places to start when trying to work on our confidence is to know where we are.

Ask yourself… which one currently prevails in your life, your confidence or your insecurity? If your friends will describe you, how do you think they will?

Open to Learning vs. Fear of Changing

The moment you open yourself to changing and embrace the possibility of acquiring the lessons and experiences – whether good and bad – you are showing a sign of confidence. You don't fear to fail since you trust yourself as well as your skills.

Accepting any forms of lessons as they come is a very powerful way to develop your confidence. The more you accept that it's okay to commit mistakes, the more you open yourself to take advice from others, and the more willing you are to take risks, the more confident you will be about yourself and your abilities. Fearing change means holding yourself back from much-needed growth that's important to improving your confidence.

Genuine vs Faking

Showing your real self is a sign of confidence. In other words, being genuine and confidence go hand in hand. You don't have to put on a mask and hide your who you truly are and adapt to what others expect you to be. Aim to love yourself and be comfortable with who you are – just don't be afraid to show it.

Trying to pretend to be someone you are not produces insecurity, and this is something that can easily be noticed by others. You may find it difficult to create healthy relationships with others since there's a level of trust that might be hard for you to reach if you keep guarding yourself against who you truly are. Everyone knows the feeling of being around someone who is pretending to be someone they are not.

Be brave and always try to be you. But do it not because you're afraid that people might judge you or not accept you, but because you love yourself and you want to be comfortable in your own skin.

Taking Risks vs. Staying in Comfort Zone

Taking risks can be really scary for many, and it's even scarier if you are someone who's not confident about his abilities. Confidence needs to be developed. It is developed every time you choose to accept your mistakes and choose to do things that are beyond your comfort zone.

Recognize your comfort zone and explore these areas a little bit more as it will allow you to also explore the insecurity that lies within you – the insecurity that is possibly holding you back from attaining your dreams.

Building People Up vs. Tearing Them Down

Dragging people down is something insecure people like doing. And this is something that becomes a bigger problem overtime – snowballing from insecurity into a total toxic behavior.

Insecurity is fueled and sustained by negativity. It's necessary in order to endure the voice at the back of your head that's telling you that you're not good enough. Without facing negativity, you'd have to face taking responsibility for your emotions and actions. You'd have to build your confidence.

By trying to motivate others and helping them acknowledge their positive qualities, you're practicing confidence within you. You're strong enough and not afraid to stand next to someone who's successful, confident, and talented.

Sees the Positive in Differences vs. Judgmental of Differences

It's so common for someone who has so much insecurity to judge other people starkly. If you're feeling insecure about a specific part of your life, then you might find yourself judging other people in this area. On the other hand, when you're confident, it's so easy to find good things in others and even hope the best for them all the time. The success of other people motivates you and it brings out the best in you.

This is commonly seen in racism, sexism, and other forms of discrimination. When someone is feeling insecure about himself because of how others are, they tend to be addicted to finding where they fit in.

Making Decision vs. Following

Most of the time, confident people tend to be good leaders. Leading their lives and even others is something that they can do well. Being a leader is something that is inherent, but it is also something that can be earned and developed. If you are a confident leader, people who follow you also become confident.

This is not to say that followers are usually the insecure ones. However, insecure individuals tend to be the ones who usually rely on other people when making decisions. If you find yourself constantly waiting for other people to make decisions for you, then perhaps you need to check on yourself as you might need to start building up your confidence.

Gives Validation vs. Seeks Validation

It's so easy for confident people to give praise and compliments to others. This is because they don't feel threatened by the goodness other people achieve.

On the other hand, when someone comes from a place of insecurity, he tends to always seek validation. A person with so much insecurity tends to feel empty and sad that he thinks that he can't fill in a void in his life if someone else does it first. This can affect relationships because the moment other people are not able to fill that void, this is something that may backfire, which makes the person may feel even more insecure.

Self-Reflection vs. Self-Rejection

Having the ability to just sit and reflect on themselves is probably something that most confident people have in common. These people have no problem asking themselves difficult questions, openly looking at the answers and then using self-development to get better in certain areas in their lives. Being alone with themselves is something that they can do without any problem.

On the other hand, insecurity can manifest in many forms of self-rejecting means. When someone acts from a place of insecurity, he is able to find different creative ways just to avoid the truth about themselves.

Looks for Help vs. Try to do Everything Alone

Confident individuals have no problem asking for help from other people. They are always open to learning new things from others and use their newly-learned skills to their advantage. They are very confident that other people's abilities and knowledge don't negate theirs.

On the other hand, those people who are insecure might act too protective of their own abilities. They tend to feel offended when someone offers help. This makes them stuck in their own ways and hinder their learning.

CHAPTER 3
BODY LANGUAGE

So, do actions really speak louder than words? Can you really rely on someone's actions better than the words they say?

Experts say that most of what we communicate is through our body language, with about 60% to 90% of the way we communicate being non-verbal. These subtle social cues do a lot by letting us truly understand other people's real thoughts and intentions.

So, how can we spot these imperative subtle social cues that explain what's really going on in people's minds?

3.1 The Different Signs to Be Aware of and What They Mean

Whether you are at home, work, or in public surrounded by family, coworkers, or strangers, people's body language speaks loudly. It has been believed that body language establishes over 60% of what people communicate, so being able to learn how to read the nonverbal cues people send is a treasured skill. From how the eyes behave to the direction wherein a person directs his feet, the body language shows what's going on in his mind. In this chapter, I will briefly explain how to analyze body language to better understand the people you interact with on day to day basis.

Study the Eyes

The way eyes behave says a lot. It's important that when you communicate with someone, you must pay attention to whether he makes direct eye contact to you or not. Inability to look someone in the eyes directly can indicate disinterest, boredom, discomfort, or even dishonesty –

especially when the person looks away. If someone looks down, on the other hand, it usually means that the person is feeling nervous or submissive. Another thing you may want to notice are the pupils. Pupils dilate every time cognitive effort goes up, so it means that if someone is fixated on someone or something they like, the pupils are automatically going to dilate. The blinking rate of a person can also indicate something about what's going on in his head. The blinking rate goes up whenever people are thinking deeply or are feeling stressed.

Gaze at the Mouth

Pay attention to the movement of the mouth when you're trying to analyze nonverbal behavior. A simple smile can a powerful gesture. As we already know, smiling is an essential nonverbal cue to be aware of. There are different kinds of smiles, which includes real smiles and fake smiles. A real smile means that the person feels happy and enjoys the company of those who are around him. On the other hand, a fake smile usually means they just want to please others by making them think he's happy but they are feeling something else. There's also the "half-smile", which is another common facial expression that only engages a side of the mouth, which can indicate uncertainty or sarcasm.

Notice the Proximity

Proximity is your distance from the other person. Take notice of how close or how far someone is standing or sitting next to you in order to determine if they view you positively. When someone is standing or sitting close to someone, then it might indicate rapport. On the other hand, if you notice someone backing up or moving away when you try to get close to them, then this might indicate discomfort. You are able to tell a lot of things about the kind of relationship two people have by simply observing the distance between them. However, you must remember that some cultures favor less or more distance throughout the interaction, so proximity isn't an accurate indicator of kinship with someone at all times.

Get a Hint from the Head Movement

The speed at which someone nods their head when you're talking may indicate the length or lack of patience. Slow nodding may indicate that the person is interested in what he's hearing and wants to hear more, while fast nodding might mean that the person has heard enough and prefer to stop listening and start talking. Tilting the head on the side while in a conversation might be an indication of interest in what he's hearing while tilting the head backward might be an indication of uncertainty or suspicion. Some people also point using their head or face at people they're interested in or share an attraction with.

Check out the Feet

Our feet are the part of our body where we usually "leak" important nonverbal cues. The reason people involuntarily send nonverbal messages through their feet is due to the fact that they're normally very focused on controlling their facial expressions and upper body resulting in showing important cues through their feet. When they are standing or sitting, a person generally points their feet where they would like to go. So, when you notice that someone's feet are directed in your direction, this could be a great indication that they have a promising opinion of you. This is usually the case for one-on-one interaction as well as group interaction.

See the Hand Signals

Just like the feet, our hands give out imperative nonverbal cues. It's an important area when trying to analyze body language, so make sure to pay attention to this part of the body. When someone is standing, see where the hands are placed. Search for specific hand gestures like where does the person places the hand, in the pocket or maybe on his face. This might specify anything from anxiety to absolute sham. Insentient pointing specified by hand gestures could also speak volumes. When executing hand gestures, a person is going to point in the general direction of the person they're sharing an affinity with.

Observe the Arm Position

You may want to see someone's arms as the doorway to their body. If someone crosses their arms while speaking to you, it's normally seen as a defensive, obstructive gesture. Crossed arms could also specify vulnerability, anxiety, or having a closed mind. If crossed arms come with a genuine smile and overall relaxed position, then it could be a sign of confidence and being laid back. When someone puts their hands on their hips, it's normally used to apply dominance and it is usually used by men more commonly than women.

Keep in mind that the tips mentioned above can provide you with an awareness of the real motives behind someone's behavior, but they are not infallible. When you're trying to analyze one's body language, you have to remember that these methods are not going to be applicable to everyone 100% of the time. There will be aspects like the person's culture and general body language habits that have to be considered in order to precisely decipher nonverbal cues.

3.2 Recognizing People's Intentions

One of the most important skills I've developed in my life is the ability to better understand intentions of other people. Just like anyone who's learning new skills, I have both thrived and failed at this a lot of times in the past. With these trials and errors, I was able to build up myself up to the level where it has become easier for me to judge intentions and motives of people much more clearly, and so their external actions hardly ever affect me emotionally.

Again, let me repeat the fact that the human's body language isn't the same to the way we express ourselves through speaking. A specific movement does not essentially signify a certain word or emotion. There is no such thing as a body language manual or dictionary that is going to help you crack the hidden meaning behind specific gestures. And the truth is, there are no hard and brief rules in terms of understanding a person's unspoken intentions. Even scientists who are trained in the skill of analyzing people make mistakes, particularly when observing someone who's capable of controlling much of their mindful physical behavior.

Gestures are vague. And if you're someone who's good at analyzing others by reading their body language, you know that a certain action can mean different things. If you see someone crossing his arms, it's wrong to accuse him of being defensive because he might be feeling something else – he could be feeling cold or just pretty tired or it could also be an indication that he's feeling comfortable. And it's also possible that the person is feeling all those things at the same time. Yes, it's possible for someone to feel tired, cold, defensive, and comfortable at the same time.

Research shows that no matter what we feel, it first shows up in our body, and then in our conscious minds. So, if we are feeling hungry, angry, happy, impatient, etc., our bodies are aware of it beforehand, and they reliably signal those feelings. Being able to analyze body language, then, is a matter of learning and understanding intents of others, and not their particular conscious thoughts.

So, in this case, how does body language reflect presentation delivery? This works by stressing the points and arguments you are making. In other words, these are the conscious adjustment of your gestures, posture, and expression that are going to underscore and emphasize everything you are trying to say.

Through this, the body language lets you add an emotional length to your presentations. Even though your good posture does not essentially signify a certain meaning, it nevertheless shows the listener something welcoming and positive.

Again, you must keep in mind that body language is not mind reading nor does it provide one an insight into what another person is trying to. All in all, when trying to analyze people's intentions carefully, body language can really be helpful.

Generally speaking, you want to focus on what people want from you when trying to figure out their intentions. However, you're not always going to be able to work out a person's exact intentions, but it is ideal to be able to figure them out in as many circumstances as possible.

3.3 How to Tell If Someone Is Attracted to You

When you're meeting someone for the first time, particularly in a romantic encounter, it's so easy to know as to whether we like them or not – but the question is, how do we know if they like us?

Well, there are some nonverbal cues that easily tell you as to whether or not someone is into you. Here are the body language ciphers you might want to look out for:

❖ **Mutual Eye Contact**

People stare at people they like and if they don't like you, they tend to avoid looking at you directly. The thing that is responsible for increased eye contact is neurochemical oxytocin. High level of oxytocin boosts mutual eye gaze and offers a sense of happiness that boosts mutual attraction. Oxytocin also upsurges pupil dilation that shows interest. The bigger the dilation, the more attracted a person feels toward another person. Throughout the last century B.C., Cleopatra, supposedly the most attractive woman during her time, dilated her pupils with atropine in order to make herself look more sensual.

There's a fine line between bigger staring and eye contact that's impolite. You are able to upsurge mutual gaze by keeping eye contact as you turn your head to disrupt the gaze; the other person doesn't observe your extended gaze as your head is turning. If the person you are with keeps eye contact with you, then there's a big possibility that they like you.

❖ **A Gentle Touch**

People usually get touchy when it comes to the person they like. In a romantic relationship, the woman might lightly touch the arm of the person they're into. However, keep in mind that this

47

gentle touch isn't an indication that they want a sexual encounter; it merely specifies she is into you. Men express their liking for the same gender by fist bumping or casually hitting the other person at the back shoulder or shoulder. Men equally express their liking for women by doing a playful physical activity. Another type of touching is tidying. Removing lint off of the clothing of another person or fixing their hair or tie might mean they like you. Touching can be a great indicator that a person is into you or not. If you casually touch another person and they snappishly pull away, the person may not like you or just don't want to be too intimate with you.

❖ Inward Leaning

A great indicator that someone you're talking to is into you is body orientation. People lean toward people they like and keep a further distance from those they don't like. Inward leaning reflects rapport. For instance, if there are two people sitting next to one another, their heads will lean toward one another. Next, their shoulders are going to turn toward one another. Furthermore, their torsos will entirely turn as they face each other. Lastly, if two people like each other, then they will lean towed each other.

❖ Mirroring

It's normal for people who like each other to mirror the body positions of each other. Mirroring is able to help develop rapport and could also be used to see whether the person you're talking with is also into you. It delivers a subconscious signal to the person you're with that you are into them; sequentially, they're inclined to like you. When meeting someone, mirror their body position. Eventually, during the encounter, change the position of the body. And if you see that the person also changes his position to mirror you, chances are, they like you.

❖ Barriers

Two people who like each other tend to remove the objects that separate them. Similarly, if two people are not into each other, they feel more comfortable having an object that separates them.

These barriers include personal items like newspapers, bags, purses, cups, books, cushions, and any common items around. Having a barrier, however, doesn't necessarily mean that the person does not like you, but it still lets you know that the rapport isn't well established yet. A glass or a cup could be used to monitor liking: If someone you are with puts their glass or cup between you two, it builds a barrier indicating that rapport hasn't yet been established. As the conversation carries, observe where the person puts their glass or cup. If they put it to his side and not in front of the two of you, then they probably like you.

Observing nonverbal behaviors lets you to see the progress of the relationship-building procedure and allows you to know if the person you're with is into you. Nonverbal behaviors also indicate that the person you like, likes interacting with you, which offers a chance for you to develop your relationship under promising conditions.

CHAPTER 4

VERBAL & PARA-VERBAL COMMUNICATION

The difference between Verbal and Para-verbal communication

Of course, you should know by now that communication is a natural phenomenon that naturally takes place between people; it's an act of interaction with people. However, communications don't only come in the form of words. Communication can be both Verbal and Non-verbal.

Verbal communication is the form of communication that uses words to exchange information in the form of speaking or writing. On the other hand, **Nonverbal communication** is the type that doesn't use words. This is done using other forms of interactions. This type of communication may take place with unspoken or unwritten messages like facial expressions, body language, sign language, and others. Now, let's compare the two types of communication to help analyze people better through the way they communicate,

BASIS FOR COMPARISON	VERBAL COMMUNICATION	NON-VERBAL COMMUNICATION
Meaning	The communication wherein the sender makes use of words to convey the message to the receiver is recognized as verbal communication.	The communication which happens between sender and receiver using signs is identified as non-verbal communication.
Types	Formal and Informal	Vocalics, Chronemics, Haptics, Proxemics, Kinesics, Artifacts.
Time Consuming	No	Yes

Probabilities of sending the wrong message	Rarely happens.	Happens often.
Documentary Proof	Yes, through voice recording or written form.	No
Advantage	Can easily be understood.	Can easily express feelings and emotions.
Presence	The message can be conveyed through phone calls, letters, etc. so the personal presence of both people does not make any change.	The personal presence of both parties to the communication is necessary.

4.1 Definition of Verbal Communication

The communication wherein the sender makes use of words – may it be spoken or written – to convey the message to the receiver is called Verbal Communication. It's the most effective type of communication which leads to the quick interchange of feedback and information. There are fewer possibilities of misunderstanding as the communication between people is usually clear.

There are two ways to send information. The first way is oral, which can be done face-to-face, phone calls, lectures, and other ways which involve voice. The second way is written, which can be done through letters, emails, text, etc.

Communication can also be categorized into two different types:

* **Formal Communication:** Also known as official communication, this is a type of communication that uses a pre-defined channel from the sender to convey the details to the receiver.

* **Informal Communication:** Mostly known as grapevine, this is a type of communication where the sender doesn't have to follow any pre-defined channels to convey the information he has to deliver.

4.2 Definition of Nonverbal Communication

Non-verbal communication is derived from the understanding of both sender and receiver to communicate, as the delivery of messages from the sender to the receiver doesn't involve words. So, if ever that the receiver knows the message entirely and good feedback is provided afterward, then the communication flourishes.

It matches the verbal communication a lot of times, in order to understand the mindset, as well as the status of the people involved but all in all, it's all an act of understanding. The forms of Non-verbal communication are as under:

- ❖ **Chronemics:** Using time in communication is chronemics, which has something to do about the receivers' or the senders' personality.

- ❖ **Vocalics:** The voice's tone, pitch, and volume used by the sender for delivering a message to the receiver are called paralanguage or vocalists.

- ❖ **Haptics:** It's a communication which involves touching. This is usually used in expressing feelings and emotions.

- ❖ **Kinesics:** It's the study of a person's body language. It includes postures, gestures, facial expressions, etc.

- ❖ **Proxemics:** This is the distance kept by a person while communicating with other people; it communicates regarding the person's relationship with others such as personal, intimate, social, and public.

- ❖ **Artifacts:** The look of a person that has to do about his personality. For example, the way he dresses, carries himself, lifestyle, etc.

Key Differences Between Verbal and Nonverbal Communication

Here are more detailed points that explain the difference between verbal and non-verbal communication:

1. Communication that involves words is known as Verbal communication, while the communication that is based on signs, is Non-verbal communication.

2. There will be less possibility of misunderstanding when verbal communication is used. On the other hand, the possibilities of confusion and misunderstanding in non-verbal communication are a lot more.

3. When it comes to verbal communication, the exchange of messages is extremely fast that leads to quick feedback. Meanwhile, the non-verbal communication is derived more from understanding that takes time and that's why it's fairly slow.

4. When it comes to verbal communication, it's not necessarily required for both parties to be present because this communication can be done even if both sides are far from each other. On the other hand, people who are involved in non-verbal communication have to be with each other.

5. In verbal communication, the documentary proof can be saved if the communication is done in a formal or written way. However, in nonverbal communication, there's no conclusive proof when it's done.

Keep in mind that Verbal and Non-verbal communication aren't contradictory to each other; instead, they're complementary. In other words, these two types of communications can even go hand in hand for a more effective human communication.

Obviously, verbal communication is an important part of life because words are still the most effective way of communication. However, just like the saying goes, "actions speak louder than words", especially for those who are not able to speak words as well as others, if not, at all – like for babies or people with speech disabilities.

4.3 How to Identify Para-verbal Communication and Language in People

Every time we hear the word "communication", the first thing that probably comes to our minds is probably spoken or written words. But between two people, communication may come in other forms! After all, being seen from the viewpoint of its evolutionary history, this word doesn't stand alone – there are other forms of communication that are also similarly important! In fact, you might have already experienced a situation where you are able to express something or understand someone by just a gaze. Or you've probably experienced talking to someone and thinking to yourself, "I'm pretty sure he's lying". In this case, then you've already used two channels people make use of when communicating with each other and that's what we are going to talk about in this subchapter.

As you probably know, communication is a big part of anyone's life – heck, even animals have their own ways of communication. When you're mad with someone, sometimes, we might choose not to talk. We could simply turn our back to them and they will know what you may want to happen – so, in some way, you did some sort of communication. Letting your body speak for you means you are non-verbally communicating. This form of communication includes different physical signals used in expressing opinions. emotions, opinions, aversion, and affections. As a rule of thumb, we use them in replacement of our verbal messages. And you probably haven't thought about it, but it's pretty easy to convey a lot of information all on its own.

Generally, using nonverbal communications is pretty quick and straightforward as they're usually made subconsciously and so, they are more genuine and spontaneous. Because of this, a nonverbal form of communication is seen more as a distinct indication of what we truly feel. This gets truly interesting when verbal and non-verbal communication just don't seem to be saying the same thing. For example, when we ask someone the question, "Are you okay?" They say they are, but their actions and facial expressions don't say that they are. In this situation, nonverbal information is seen as more essential and reliable compared to verbal information. This is where the saying that goes "Actions speak louder than words" comes into the picture.

Here are some important fundamentals of nonverbal communication:

- ❖ Distance
- ❖ Gestures and facial expressions
- ❖ Line of vision
- ❖ Objects
- ❖ Posture

Along with the verbal and non-verbal information, there's another means of communicating I want you to be aware of: the para-verbal. This form of communication has all the signals when it comes to dealing with voice modulation and level.

You're probably already aware of this form of communication, and if not, then you should be. When we're certain of ourselves, feel confident, and calm, our voice tends to sound clear and well-articulated. For example, if we feel nervous or aggressive, we tend to speak fast, loud, and high-pitched. Anger and aggression usually make the voice louder. On the other hand, sadness and insecurity manifests itself by a rather more subdued and a higher tone or also by wallowing. Along with insecurity, the level of voice can also express happiness and excitement – you possibly have shrieked for happiness when something really nice happens. On the other hand, fear could naturally lead to some extremely remarkable squealing. As our emotions or feelings change, so does the way we speak.

At present, para-verbal signals aren't completely unambiguous; the subjects of the experiment most easily identify the emotions anger and fear based on the level of voice. From an evolutionary standpoint, this easily makes sense as it was definitely extremely useful that a person was conscious of a danger the other person had noticed in advance or when a person was furious, and so it might be safer to keep distance or to avoid an impending argument. Along with these emotional details, para-verbal signs also give information when it comes to which group we belong to. For example, which dialect we speak or where our accent came from.

When you feel in doubt, para-verbal signals are definitely superior when it comes to verbal content: when someone tells you he's not afraid of you but says it in a trembling voice, two octaves higher than normal, there's a high chance that he's not telling the truth. Lie researchers have concluded that para-verbal signals could be an extremely effective indication of conscious attempts to lie or deceive people. The wrong modulation, conflicting intonation, or incorrect emphasis immediately warn experts that someone isn't telling the whole truth.

Even though opinions about the reliability of para-verbal and nonverbal signals as a part of communication vary – there's no doubt that these two areas showcase any number of opportunities for misunderstandings and misinterpretation. However, all experts agree to the fact that we impulsively mark the value of para-verbal and nonverbal signals significantly higher than the one of verbal signals. Derived from a research, nonverbal and para-verbal fundamentals showcase about 60% to 90% in response to the question whether a person was telling the truth or not.

If you find this subject interesting, then you'd find this quick exercise fun and useful:

- ❖ The next time you get the chance to talk to someone, pay close attention to your conversation to their non- and para-verbal signals. What captures your attention the most? Are there specific individuals within your close circle who tend to show incongruent behavior more than others? What do you think is the reason behind this?

- ❖ Try out the influence you have on others, for example, every time you hold your head up and stare directly into the eyes or contrasted with often casting your eyes on something else and slightly tilting your head forward, what kind of reactions do other people give you that you can easily notice?

- ❖ Whenever you feel stressed out or insecure, deliberately pay attention to your hands. They usually show the first sign of betrayal whenever you don't feel up to par by fiddling with something or subconsciously touching other parts of our body. If this is something you want to avoid, then find a subject you are able to "hold on to" giving yourself a chance to calm down.

- ❖ The next time you're going to a bar or anywhere with many people, look at a few people. Notice how you interpret their posture whenever they're taking some sort of actions or movement. Do you think they feel like they're having fun? Do they look bored, tired, uninterested, or bothered? What made you think about those emotions? It is similarly exciting to see people who are trying to flirt? Just for fun, look around and guess which couples might potentially end up being together or having their second date. This could also be a fun thing to do when you are with a friend or two.

- ❖ If the opportunity arises, it could be quite fun to watch yourself in a video while doing so, you will surely find a lot of things that are interesting!

There are four zones of "personal distance" around people recognized by communication experts. These zones are usually reserved for different types of people:

- ❖ 50 cm - extremely familiar people might get extremely close to us (50 cm).

- ❖ 50 cm to 1.2 meters - people we know pretty well; this can be considered as the intimate zone.

- ❖ 2.5 meters to 3.5 meters - acquaintances and friends where contact stays impersonal and superficial.

- ❖ 3.5 - other people and strangers

If ever somebody who does not belong there happens to go invade our "intimate zone" or even a few centimeters, for example, in overcrowded places, inside an elevator, bus, or concerts, it might make us feel uncomfortable and we try different ways to add distance from these intruders. You will have a lot of chance to do some experiment with your zone. Which distances do you find to be acceptable and those that bother you? Who do you allow to get closer to you? Is there a gender you are more comfortable with? If you want, you can also try to see what happens if you try to intrude into the "intimate zone" of another person – see how they would react.

CHAPTER 5
UNDERSTANDING EMOTIONS

It's a normal thing for us, humans, to read each other's emotions. After all, how many times have you been asked "Are you mad?" by people? If you answer, "Nothing, this is just how I am," people strangely assume that you're actually mad.

But these questions are commonly asked because people actually care about others, especially the ones that are important to them. What do these emotions mean and how are they going to affect us? Do they like us or not? Do we have to do something or just let it be?

The question that usually follows on this extremely practical worry about the feelings of other people is more logical. Perhaps, it comes first at that moment when someone responds to an event amazes you since it is different from the one you currently have.

You're wondering… "Are we feeling the same thing right now?" Which leads to a question that is more general, "Do humans experience or feel the same things as other humans?"

Philosophy has found different answers throughout the years, but in general, the conclusion is that, in general, we are disproportionate with one another. That is a mouthful, but it just means that your experience could be differently from others. Perhaps, I cared more about something and others don't, and that's normal.

Pushing forward, consider individual words. For example, if I say, "Paris" to you, you almost certainly get a mental image of this beautiful city, but what's it based on? Have you ever been to Paris before? I have, so I am definitely more familiar with the city. However, for someone who lives there, the picture of the city in his head will be inevitably more rich, detailed, and a lot more meaningful. The word alone might remind them of their favorite restaurant, their usual bus stop, the office they work at, the park they walk their dogs in, and so on.

Can you say the word "Paris" and mean the same thing to everyone? Not really.

And yet, neuroscience teaches us that people are more alike than are different. For example, recent work on brain scans is able to read human emotions with 90% accuracy. Studies showed people pictures of hostile things – hate groups, physical injuries, and acts of aggression – and it showed how people reacted predictably. But beyond that, their reactions are pretty much the same in terms of brain patterns.

In the same way, a team of psychologists at Princeton University discovered that when a storyteller and a listener come together, the patterns of their brain match up identically. This is to say that stories take over our brains similarly.

Based on brain patterns, human emotions are the same. As the lead researcher, Dr. Luke Chang puts it, human emotions have a "neural signature" that is basically the same among humans. This also shows that computers can possibly learn to identify these emotions with an accuracy of 90%.

And there is one further inference, which is that computer accuracy rate is much higher compared to what humans can manage. And here's more – it is higher even than humans are able to manage *their very own emotions*. We are not even very good when it comes to recognizing our own emotions.

Analyzing other peoples' emotions and also our own is important for great communication. That the study suggests that we're more similar than different shows that humans can lucratively learn to be more accurate when it comes to recognizing emotions and that the results may reimburse in better communications for anyone who tries it.

How to analyse the feelings of others?

Some conversations can get emotional. Even though you have good intentions, you might possibly hurt someone else's feelings without you knowing it. Listening to other people's feelings is one of the best ways to be sensitive with what they feel and to speak to them nicely. It's essential to learn different ways to deal with your own feelings too.

Recognizing Social Cues About Emotions

1. **Observe the person's face.** As you might expect, the face is the most expressive part of the body. If you are trying to know whether a person is happy, sad, lonely, upset, bored, angry, or in pain, you can start by looking at their face carefully.

   ❖ Unlike other social cues, there are seven basic facial expressions that are believed to be universal in expression throughout all cultures. These expressions are surprise, joy, contempt, disgust, anger, fear, and sadness.

   ❖ Facial expressions change quickly and might communicate multiple emotions at the same time. For instance, a person's face might show both fear and amusement if something extremely surprising has ensued.

2. **Be aware of the signs of sadness.** When a person is sad, the face will show it easily. It would not look like a cartoon-drawn picture with his smile showing upside-down, but it will show the corners of his lips to be somewhat drawn down and the jaw comes up.

   ❖ The inner sides of the person's eyebrows are going be pulled slightly inner and up to the forehead.

   ❖ Search for the skin below the eyebrows to look somewhat triangulated, with the inner corner going up.

3. **Be familiar with signs of fear.** Being aware of when someone is afraid can help you change your very own behavior. When a person is afraid, his mouth will likely be held open with his lips a little stretched as well as drawn back. His brows are normally high and strained together in one straight line.

   ❖ Check out his forehead, and search for wrinkles in the middle of the brows, not across.

❖ If a person is feeling afraid, his upper eyelid tends to rise, while the lower lid might be tensed. You will see the upper white of their eye, but the lower might not be visible.

4. **Observe the movement of the body and posture.** Indications that someone is tired might include collapsing shoulders and slackly held limbs. If someone is feeling defensive, you might notice how he may shake his head or cross his hands. If you are aware of these cues, you will be more mindful of the feelings of another person.

❖ If you are not sure if you are analyzing the body language of another person correctly, it is normally fine to ask the person vocally.

❖ But then again, if someone himself is not aware of what he is communicating, you might hear from him that everything is fine when it really is not.

5. **Consider the vocal tone.** Some people naturally moderate the tone of their voice to match the size of the room in order to be heard. If you happen to be in a big room, and the person is talking loudly, it is likely that he is simply trying to be heard. But the use of the same vocal tone in such little space can be a sign of anger, frustration, or even fear.

❖ If someone is having a difficult time to talk, there is a high chance that he's feeling upset or sad.

❖ If he is speaking in an excessively coherent way, then it's possible that he is being sarcastic. Because sarcasm is a means of teasing, it might specify that he's angry but trying to not to make it obvious.

5.1 How to Tell If Someone Has Had A Bad Past and Experiences

All of us have a past, but if someone is going through a childhood trauma well into adulthood, this could be a sign of a bigger issue, particularly in terms of relationships. The influence of childhood on future relationships can be pretty strong, so unless there is some kind of resolution, they may encounter some horrible consequences that may also hold them back from building a healthy, strong relationship.

In my line of work, I constantly encounter people with feeling their absolute best selves, where they can feel comfortable and content in both present and future relationships. An initial step towards having this outlook is to overcome any hindrances you may face in the way, and those can usually be found from the memories of your past or your childhood. If you notice that someone gets too sensitive on a certain subject due to what happened during their childhood, you can try to talk to them about it or encourage them to seek help from a therapist. Through this, they may find a solution that will bring them a feeling of inner peace to move along with their life. The moment they decide to let go, it will be easier for them to put all their energy in their present and future self, and be open and accepting of what life has to offer. Below are the 9 signs a person's childhood has affected his present and future relationships.

1. Insecure Attachment Style to Parents

Mandy Kopplers, a CBT therapist, said that if someone was raised with an insecure style of attachment, they will be more fearful and agitated of having relationships. Adults who carry insecure attachments are likely to be emotionally unstable in relationships. There are some who even have personality disorders with extremely firm, black and white attitude when it comes to relationships with other people. There usually are no grey areas and this has normally developed to pay off for fear of abandonment or rejection. People with an insecure attachment are usually super vigilant to any possible types of abandonment and rejections.

2. Making Present-Day Decisions Based on the Past

After having to deal with a devastating illness, I learned a lot about myself. My main discovery has been the fact that throughout the years, I've been making decisions derived from the labels that were provided to me, or that I believed when I was younger. And this is something I also saw on people who had a problem in their childhood.

3. Trust Issues

It is said that if you find it hard to trust new relationships, this might mean that you are holding onto problems you had experienced in the past. For people who had a dark past, they usually find it scary to open up to other people, always scared that their partner will cheat on them because they experienced it in the past and refuse to believe others when they say that things are all indications of trust issues. They constantly find the need to check their partner's phone or social media accounts and when they find that their partner is paying attention to others, it affects them significantly. The concept of trust is a little hard for them to swallow.

4. Being Mean to Others

Do you notice that every time someone feels upset or anxious, it becomes automatic for them to put other people down? This could be their defense mechanism to make other people feel as bad as them.

5. Too Defensive to People

When they say something offensive to others or do something that makes someone feel bad, they choose not to apologize, rather, they say something that will justify their actions, no matter how much more offensive it might be for others. They find it hard to acknowledge other people's feelings because they might have not experienced being acknowledged for how they felt in the past.

6. Always Leaving First

Constantly leaving relationships could also be a sign of being stuck in a dark past or having a childhood trauma. If you find that someone is constantly looking for reasons to leave and are normally the one to break up a relationship, it may be a sign of having a dark past. The reason for this could be partner or parent's abandonment. So, in order for them to avoid the pain, they find the need to subconsciously abandon or leave first before anyone can do so. They hate the painful feeling of being abandoned but they have no problem making others feel that pain.

7. Being Too Demanding

This negative trait could originate from not being seen and honored as a child. Kids that were put aside or treated unimportantly by their parents as a kid tend to hold onto this fact as they grow into adults. And this unmet desire leads to deep wounding, which puts huge pressure on not just a future partner, but also in future kids.

8. Having A Hard Time to Show Real Self

If you know someone who feels uneasy to express their own thoughts and showing who they truly are, it might possibly mean that they never get the kind of acceptance they need growing up, and up to adulthood, they find themselves searching for approval. A big sign of this is having a hard time to express their real feelings or even be themselves since they were never familiar with an actual parent-child relationship that involves the exchange of feelings, or they were constantly shut down by a strict parent.

9. Parent Went Through a Mental Illness

While this is not the case all the time, if the parents happen to have gone through a mental illness, like bipolar disorder, for example, while they were growing up, they might have been exposed to unstable feelings or a rough, pebbly environment, and people in the past.

5.2 The Best Approach for Handling the Different Emotions

Not long ago, someone I am very close with told me I'm emotionally unstable. Well, I can't say he's wrong. I admit that my emotions can be too hard to handle sometimes, in fact, even for me. I have always been an emotionally-charged individual, and I don't think it's going to go away anytime soon.

While being emotional is something I have no problem with, there are times when other people, who are not as emotional as I, would find it difficult to deal with me. I'm aware that it is probably difficult to know the right thing to say when I am having bursts of emotions, but then again, there are several things that people say that are just not helpful.

Here are some dos and don'ts to remember when having to deal with emotional people:

DON'T: Tell them they are being too emotional.

Well, I'm going to bet that they probably know that. After all, being emotional doesn't come overnight. Most of the time, it has been a part of their personality since they were infants. Calling them emotional wouldn't do anything well. In fact, it might make them even more emotional.

DO: Ask them what they feel.

Of course, they are being emotional, but there are surely reasons why. And you want to try to figure out how they exactly feel. If ever they decide to reveal it to you, it will help them reflect, which, sequentially, might help them feel a little better, at least.

DON'T: Say you understand what they feel when you don't

The truth is, you would not always understand every emotion people experience, and it's okay. It doesn't mean there is something wrong with you. Each person feels differently. By saying that you know how they feel even though you clearly don't, they might feel like you are simply trying to dismiss their feelings as soon as possible because you don't want to deal with them.

No one would like to feel like their emotions or problems are not important.

DO: Say that you want to know and understand how they feel

They might probably tell you that you don't get it, and that's pretty acceptable. At least you told them that you are interested and open to hearing what they feel. There's a good chance that it will make them feel better.

DON'T: Get mad

For someone who's not very emotional, hearing someone cry easily can be pretty frustrating. Being frustrated is alright, but as much as possible, you may want to try not to be obviously upset. By doing so, you'll just make them feel more emotional, but it could also just make everything worse.

Emotional people are emotional – it's not something they can easily control and manipulate. Don't get mad at them; they're probably mad enough with themselves.

DO: Say it's okay

This simple word might come up as cliché. However, emotional people tend to think that there's something wrong with them and it's not okay. Excessive emotions are usually seen as negative, and so, they tend to get mad with themselves when they cannot adapt to this false standard.

Tell them it is okay, and there's no point of getting mad at themselves. They may say that you don't understand them at first, but hearing someone tell you "it's okay" and it's going to be okay does a big thing in making you feel better. Sometimes, validation just does something really big.

DON'T: Try to fight emotion using logic

Logically, yes, they're probably acting silly. Sure, perhaps you have a seamlessly logical solution to their problem that is causing them to be too emotional. However, by trying to fix everything using your incredible logical solution, you're probably just going to make things even worse.

Their emotional state is probably not ready for logical reasoning. Emotions aren't normally logical. On top of this, they are probably not looking for a solution. Instead, they might probably need someone who will listen to them.

DO: Acknowledge that you might not be the best person to help them

Even though you know you can, it's probably better to say that you can't help them. Tell them you might not be able to be helpful in fixing their problem right away, but you are always ready to listen and what they feel is important. Honestly, someone to listen is probably just what they need.

DON'T: Say that it's no big deal

Of course, this is a big deal! Maybe for you, it is not, but for others, what they are experiencing might be affecting all aspects of their life. It's definitely a big deal, although later on, it might be less of a big deal when they start to calm down. When they are at peak of their emotion, it could mean everything to them.

DO: Check in with them later to know how they feel

The fact that you let know that you care about them enough to ask about their emotional challenges and troubles, regardless of how silly they might sound, will mean a lot to them. You, checking back to them will make them feel important, which may even help them when dealing with certain emotions in the future.

DON'T: Talk them down

Don't think that when someone is being too emotional, they are acting like a child. This could be one of the worst things you can tell to someone who is feeling too much emotion. Talking down to people will just make them feel even more upset. So, try not to be a jerk and treat them the way you want to be treated – with respect.

DO: Show a little emotion

Show them that it's normal to feel emotion. Even though you have the emotional capacity of a zombie, just try as much as you can.

Don't be afraid to show that you can also be a bit emotional sometimes. You don't have to pretend to be as emotional as them. A little bit of emotion can do wonder in making them feel they are not alone with the challenges they are currently facing.

CHAPTER 6
PERSONALITY TYPES

So, the magic question that many of us want an answer to is… What really makes a person who they are?

Every person has a unique trait that you can't easily find in others. Experts are trying to figure out the science behind people's personality with individual differences in the way they think, feel, and act.

There are a lot of ways to measure one's personality, but experts have generally given up on dividing humanity precisely into different types. Instead, they concentrate on a person's personality traits.

Five of the most widely accepted of these traits are:

* ❖ Openness
* ❖ Conscientiousness
* ❖ Agreeableness
* ❖ Extraversion
* ❖ Neuroticism

Conveniently, you are able to remember these traits using the abbreviation of OCEAN, or if you want, CANOE works too.

A team of experts developed the list of traits in the 1970s. This team of two was led by Robert R. McCrae and Paul Costa of the National Institutes of Health and Lewis Goldberg and Warren Norman of the University of Michigan at Ann Arbor.

These traits are the elements that make up the personality of every individual. A person may have a dash of honesty, a great amount of conscientiousness, a standard level of extraversion, adequate openness, and nearly no neuroticism at all. Or you could just be conscientious, neurotic, disagreeable, introverted, and barely open to anything at all. Here is what each trait in this Big Five entails:

Openness

Openness refers to being open to the experience. Individuals who have a high level of openness enjoy what life has to offer. They are inquisitive, imaginative, and know how to appreciate art and new things.

On the other hand, those individuals who have a low level of openness are simply the opposite: They would rather cling to their old habits, try to dodge new experiences, and possibly are not the most adventurous person. It's not easy, if not impossible, for many to change their personality, and this also doesn't happen overnight. However, openness is a personality trait that has been shown to be subject to change as the person gets old.

Conscientiousness

Those who are conscientious are the ones you would normally label as organized and carry a strong sense of responsibility. These people are usually dependable, well-organized, and always have their eyes on the prize. You would not be able to find conscientious people going on adventures on over the world journeys with just their backpack; they are into planning and figuring out what to expect before their trip.

Those who are low in conscientiousness could be expected to be more freewheeling and impulsive. They might tend toward being careless. Conscientiousness is a great trait for a person to have, as it has been connected to accomplishment in school and job.

Extraversion

Extraversion against introversion might be the most identifiable personality trait in the list. The higher the extraversion of a person is, the more outgoing they are. Signs of being extrovert are being sociable, talkative, and being the light of a party. These people tend to be self-confident and cheery throughout social interactions.

On the other hand, there is the introversion that is the opposite of it. These people might require a lot of time alone. Maybe this is because their brains process social interaction in a different way. Introversion is usually confused with being shy and antisocial, but these descriptions are way, way different. Being shy may imply a fear of being in social interactions or an incapacity to function outside their comfort zone. Actually, it's not that introverts can't do well during social interactions; it's just that they mostly prefer not to be in a situation or they like choosing the people they are going to be interacting with.

Agreeableness

Agreeableness measures the level of kindness and warmth of a person. The more agreeable a person is, the more they are likely to be trustworthy, compassionate, and helpful. On the other hand, disagreeable people are usually the ones we label as cold and distrustful of others, and you might have a hard time cooperating with them.

Neuroticism

In order to truly understand neuroticism, you can watch George Costanza of the American sitcom called "Seinfeld." The fictional character, George, is known for his neuroses, which the show explains to be rooted in his dysfunctional parents. He's the kind of person who worries about everything, get anxious a lot over germs and disease, and even quit his job because his anxiety of not having access to a private bathroom is too much for him to handle.

George might be high when it comes to the scale of neuroticism. However, this is a real personality trait. Individuals with neuroticism worry a lot and easily slip into depression and anxiety. It's so easy for these people to find things to worry about.

On the other hand, those who are low in neuroticism level tend to be emotionally stable and think more rationally.

As expected, neuroticism is associated with a lot of bad health conditions. Compared to emotionally stable individuals, neurotic people tend to die younger, possibly for the reason that they turn to drugs, alcohol, and smoking to ease their nerves.

But that's not only it. Perhaps, the creepiest thing about neuroticism is that parasites could be the culprit why some people experience these things. And no, I don't mean the natural anxiety that might come with knowing that a tapeworm has been living in your body. A 2006 study shows that undetected infection by the parasite called *Toxoplasma gondii* might be the reason why some people are prone to neuroticism.

Other personality measures

Even though personality types have gotten out of favor in the modern psychological study as too reductive, they are still well-used by career counselors and in the business world in order to help them form people's understanding of themselves. Maybe the most known is the Myers-Briggs Type Indicator, in fact, you might be even familiar with this.

Myers-Briggs Type Indicator is a questionnaire derived from the work of early psychologist Carl Jung, which sorts people into certain categories derived from four areas: sensation, intuition, feeling, and thinking; and also, two attitudes: extraversion and introversion.

Intuition and sensing refer to how we prefer to collect information about the world, whether it is through sensing or concrete information or intuition or emotional feelings. Feeling and thinking refer to how we choose our decisions. The thinking types tend to run with logic, while the feeling types tend to base decisions on their emotions.

The Myers-Briggs system is made of the judging/perception contradiction, which defines how individuals choose to deal with the world around them. Judging types take decisive action, while perceiving people would rather choose open options. The system identifies 16 personality types derived on the four traits and two attitudes. The 16 different types are the following:

- ❖ The Composer – ISFP Personality
- ❖ The Inspector – ISTJ Personality
- ❖ The Counselor – INFJ Personality
- ❖ The Mastermind – INTJ Personality
- ❖ The Giver – ENFJ Personality
- ❖ The Craftsman – ISTP Personality
- ❖ The Provider – ESFJ Personality
- ❖ The Idealist – INFP Personality
- ❖ The Performer – ESFP Personality
- ❖ The Champion – ENFP Personality
- ❖ The Doer – ESTP Personality
- ❖ The Supervisor – ESTJ Personality
- ❖ The Commander – ENTJ Personality
- ❖ The Thinker – INTP Personality
- ❖ The Nurturer – ISFJ Personality
- ❖ The Visionary – ENTP Personality

Using Myers-Briggs has always been controversial. Research suggests these types don't correlate very *well with abilities or job satisfaction.*

But can personality change?

Possibly. A 2017 study by Psychological Bulletin synthesized 207 published research claimed that one can change his personality with the help of therapy. But then again, this is unlikely to happen overnight, according to a study researcher and a social and personality psychologist at the University of Illinois, Brent Roberts. But he also said that if you really want to concentrate on one part of yourself, and you are willing to go at it analytically, there is now amplified optimism that you are able to affect change in that area.

6.1 Introvert vs Extrovert: Know the Difference

Introversion and Extroversion are two personality traits that are based on specific characteristics. When someone is reserved and doesn't open up easily, chances are, he has an introvert personality. On the other hand, when someone doesn't fear to be a social butterfly, is comfortable in being talkative, and can easily make friends, then there's a huge chance that he is extrovert.

We are the same species with different personalities. It's easy to see the fact that we are the same humans in nature, mind, body, thoughts, emotions, yet we are all unique in our own different ways. It is true what they say, there are really no two people alike, the same way as to how we think, how we feel, and the way we act are different from others, which embodies our overall personality. Now let me give you a breakdown on these two specific attitudes in order for you to know the differences between the two.

Introvert Explained

This is a personality trait where a person is interested in his mental self. Introverted individuals are naturally reserved, as they tend to be preoccupied with their own feelings and thoughts. So, it means that they tend to desire more time within their own private space. In other words, this kind of people feels comfortable and more energized when they're by themselves. So, they choose solitary activities over social interaction and some of the activities they tend to enjoy include writing, reading, listening to music, and making anything related to art. They run a world of fantasies, feelings, and the like.

A lot of people misinterpret introverts and think that they are just being shy and antisocial, but the truth is most introverts enjoy socializing and they are great listeners. They hardly approach people first and they tend to have social anxiety when surrounded by people they don't know.

Extrovert Explained

Extrovert refers to human's attitude wherein a person always like to be surrounded by people. They're confident in a social environment and are very opinionated and straightforward. You can tell that they are the complete opposite of introverts.

Extroverts tend to focus on practical realities instead of feelings and emotions, so being in solitude bores them. So, they choose to be more social, informal, practical, and enthusiastic. Furthermore, their communication skills are outstanding. People who have this kind of personality love social gatherings and being the center of attention is something they enjoy.

As you can see, it's not difficult to distinguish the difference between an introvert and extrovert. While an introvert is not into social gatherings and loves spending time alone, an extrovert, on the other hand, feels pleasure in being socially active, and easily susceptible to being bored when isolated. Furthermore, the introverts are quiet and enjoy listening more while introverts love talking more and being in the limelight.

CHAPTER 7
BEHAVIOUR ANALYSIS

Have you ever given thoughts to how fascinating human nature is? And with the fast-paced life we have, offered by the digital world, understanding the behaviors of other people has become more and more interesting and diverse.

Here, we are giving you some insights on how understanding human behavior helps improve your professional and personal lives alike.

Take a look at human behavior…

For many, it is highly beneficial to gain understanding of their own behavior and thinking in order to gain a better understanding of people around them. Being aware of the reason why someone might be having a hard time with social interactions, or is having difficulty managing emotions such as sadness and fear is something that will be highly beneficial for you when learned fully. The benefits it offers when it comes to promoting positive wellbeing are also numerous.

A level that reinforces you

A lot of careers can benefit from a background that involves reading someone's behavior as this level can help to reinforce the applicant's interpersonal skills like empathy, compassion, as well as motivation. Some of the jobs that might require these skills include the following:

❖ Child protection

❖ Community health services

❖ Human resources

❖ Support services

Making a positive change

Individuals who have a strong yearning to help other people and make use of their skills and knowledge to change the lives of others positively to help other people thrive in behavioral studies.

Learning how to analyze people's behavior gives us a wealth of information when it comes to human behavior while touching on other parts of the psychology discipline.

7.1 How to Identify and Interpret the Different Types

The way people behave differently makes them unique. And the way we act says so much about who we are. In psychology, our noticeable acts are known as behavior. However, what many people don't know is that behavior comes with different types. Psychology classifies behavior as Overt behavior, Covert behavior, Conscious behavior, Unconscious behavior, Rational behavior, Irrational behavior, Voluntary behavior, and Involuntary behavior, and that's what we are going to talk about in this subchapter.

1. Overt Behavior

This type of behavior is a person's noticeable act. It's pretty obvious that you are able to see it and even measure it at some point. Examples of this type of behavior includes jogging, eating, writing, singing, dancing, exercising, reading, studying, cleaning, etc. You got it. Regardless of what overt behavior it is, it's something that you can observe.

2. Covert Behavior

If overt behavior is something you can observe, covert behavior is a complete opposite. Instead of actions, covert behavior has something to do with one's thoughts. A person may showcase desirable acts like saying he's fine when he's not. Another example of covert behavior is insecurity.

Someone might wear a mask using this attitude. A person with this behavior can easily show different faces in different situations when they want to. This is why finding someone's true personality can sometimes be so challenging. One good example of this is a relationship; many relationships don't last because the partner finds out some untruthfulness about their partner's personality. And most of the time, this is something that can only be learned after years of being together.

3. Conscious Behavior

Conscious behavior refers to someone's intended acts. It's something that you intentionally do. A great example of this is eating a meal or taking a shower. You do these behaviors because you have to. Taking a shower, for example, is necessary before going to work. And eating a meal is of course, important to give yourself some nourishment. These behaviors are consistent with a specific purpose.

4. Unconscious Behavior

Unconscious behaviors are actions that run inevitably without controlling them with your mind. For example, breathing is something we do even when we still and our mind is resting. You might not know what kind of response you will give during a frightening situation. You don't like spiders. They freak you out when you feel them crawling on your skin. Screaming or jumping would be your unconscious response. This is something you didn't even think about.

5. Rational behavior

This category is a type of behavior in psychology that we are able to see among people on a daily basis. It refers to making the decision and actions based on existing social practices and norms. We follow rules because we need to follow them as a responsible citizen. Or we try not to do crimes because it's just something that we should not do. These behaviors are derived from the rationality that we developed to fit in the society we live in.

6. Irrational Behavior

Irrational behaviors are the actions that diverge from what is right. Normally, these behaviors are ridiculous. They don't really serve any purpose. For example, kicking a cat that's walking in front of you in absence of any particular reason.

7. Voluntary Behavior

Voluntary behaviors occur out of the free will. It's the outcome of having the authority to make decisions. You are able to take the course you want in college or just not go to school at all. You are able to focus on working and not let procrastination get the best of you. You can apply for the job you want or leave the job you hate.

8. Involuntary behavior

These behaviors are normally something out of control such as sneezing or the blinking of your eyes when light hurt them. These are the things that you do because you didn't have the chance to stop those behaviors.

In psychology, these types of behavior occur to us on a daily basis. You are able to feel these or observe them in other people. Being open to these types of behavior can be really helpful in analyzing people.

7.2 How to Identify the Different Types of Behaviour and Handle Them

When meeting a sarcastic person for the first time who always criticizes people around him, we will get an impression that he is a plain mean human being. But chances are, there might be a deeper reason for this behavior. What if he acts like that because he feels inferior and he feels like the only way for him to feel superior is to criticize others and make them feel smaller.

When trying to understand the behaviors of others, judging a person based on certain situations rather than linking his behavior to the underlying reasons could be one of the biggest mistakes you can commit.

Understanding people's behavior

Did you have that person in your school who cried after a test because he "only" got 9 correct answers out of 10 questions? You probably thought that he was silly or weird for getting upset with that. But what if he was taught as a kid that being imperfect makes him not good enough and that's a thought he carried until he grew up?

In order to fully understand someone's behavior, you should know that all types of behavior serve an extremely important role to maintain the psychological balance of the person even though the behavior might seem weird.

When parents neglect a child, that child can possibly develop a strange behavior like bullying and stealing. People freak out finding out a kid steals or bully, but do we actually consider why they developed these odd behaviors?

An essential part in understanding the behavior of others is understanding that if the person stopped from doing a certain behavior that helps him keep his psychological balance, then he is likely to develop an entirely different behavior that provides him with the same goal.

For example, if you stop a kid from stealing or if you tell him that stealing is bad, then he can possibly develop a specific type of physical illness with the goal of seizing the lost attention back. For a lot of children who have speech impediment, their stammering can be no more than just a cry for help with the intention of grabbing attention.

Using these examples, we are able to conclude that trying to fix the behaviors of others is all about looking for the reasons that drive them to execute such behavior.

How to Properly Understand People's Behavior

So, is there any specific formula we are able to follow in order to understand other people's behavior?

Well, there are, and they are listed below:

1. Try not to judge someone's behavior without considering their reasons behind those behaviors.
2. The way someone behaves during different situations is going to give an idea of his real intention. For example, someone is talkative because he is planning to run in politics, so he wants to capture people's attention. Or someone shops for expensive things because he wants to be popular.
3. It's impossible to understand someone's behavior before understanding their psychological initiatives. These initiatives are usually formed during their early childhood and are generally kept secret but the good thing is that by connecting the dots, it's not going to be too difficult to learn these initiatives.

CHAPTER 8

PSYCHOLOGY 101

Learning the ability to analyze or read people truly goes a long way. This is especially true if you want to understand or learn the real idea of what someone you're interacting with might have to do with both of your personal or professional life.

People in different professions get training on how they can analyze someone. The obvious roles that need these skills include those in psychology or the ones that are related to health and social services. But there are a lot of other jobs that use different means on how to analyze people. This arrays from salespeople to policemen. Having the ability to analyze others involves paying attention to the smallest details. You have to be able to understand both verbal and non-verbal messages and signs in others.

We all send out a lot of information through the way we move, speak, and act during certain situations. The words we say don't always reflect what we really feel. If you're thinking that being able to read people is only about being able to read what's in someone's mind and see their auras, well, think again! It's not really all about mind reading and knowing what's going on in people's mind. In fact, it's more about being deeply observant. It's about being aware of what body language you need to pay attention to and when.

8.1 FBI's Ways of Analyzing People

It may not come as a surprise for you to that criminal investigators like FBI agents use a combination of psychological, observational, and analytical methods to analyze people. More commonly known as profiling, this process examines through suspects and criminals. If you are a fan of crime TV shows, then you've likely seen this procedure dramatized. But how accurate are they in real life? Well, you can read these real techniques FBI uses and do the comparison yourself.

❖ **Baselines:** There are habits and mannerism that people use on a regular basis. They might be the norm for them, but they might indicate other things to other people. This includes habits such as constant tapping of arms, the crossing of arms, and clearing of the throat. If it is only a specific behavior that can be considered as a quirk, it generates part of their baseline. Other aspects or extreme repetition of actions might show that they're uncomfortable, nervous, or anxious.

❖ **Differences:** The moment you become aware of a person's baseline or normal behavior, spotting the difference would be easier. These usually show up throughout interaction with others. You can start comparing how they're interacting with you, with others, and how do they behave with several people in the room. They also see how consistent their behavior is and how or if they change over time.

❖ **Voices and Language:** The way people talk definitely say a lot of things about them. FBI pays attention to the tone and volume of a person's voice. They notice every word they say, style of language, and jargon they use. Being about to hear analyze the strength or conviction of a person's words can usually say more about the person's thoughts compared to the volume of their voice.

❖ **Movement:** See how people move when they're walking. Do they shuffle their arms? How do they position their feet? Where do they place their hands? Do they walk fast? How about the way they stand? Do they slouch or do they look confident?

❖ **Clusters:** One type of movement, action, or speaking on its own may not say something out of ordinary. But repeating one movement over and over again or seeing different non-verbal cues taking place all at the same time might. A body that shows this cluster may interpret someone who's feeling anxious or nervous. They might be sweating, fidgeting, and muttering all at once.

❖ **Reflections:** There are times when we unconsciously mirror or mimic back the facial expressions or emotions we see in other people. Imitating happens when we're feeling comfortable being around with someone, but also when we are not. When we see someone smiling, smiling seems like an automatic thing to do. When someone laughs, we laugh.

When someone's looking sad, we tend to show the same emotion. This is something that people can fake, but usually, they mean well.

- ❖ **Personalities**: Being aware of people's basics personality traits is a must. This is where the two types usually play a part – are they introverted or extroverted? It's also important to be aware of their decision-making process, what makes them motivated. The way people make decisions and deal with stress and risks can say so much about them and how their mind works.

Psychology Tricks to Analyzing People

Anyone trained in the art of analyzing people's behavior learns and makes use of tricks gathered from psychology. The strategies and skills described in the previous section are essential. This includes having the capability to understand different personality types, find a baseline, search clusters, understand body language and movement, mimicking, and observing how people talk.

In order to have an accurate analysis of other people, you must also know at least a little psychology about yourself too! This includes the following:

Being Aware of Your Biases

In order to analyze other people accurately, you must be aware of your own biases. Your biases are able to affect your judgment. All of us have them. The secret is to be able to know how we can reflect on them and also put them aside while you're trying to analyze someone. By doing that, you stay objective and neutral. For instance, it's human nature to feel empathy or attraction to people who have the same experiences or situations as you.

Making the Most of Your Intuition

Our gut feelings or intuition, no matter what you want to call it, is usually pretty accurate. Never underestimate your capability to analyze a person or a certain situation by trusting in your emotions and especially your instinct. First impressions are very powerful. Most of the time, what we think of someone for the first time is accurate. But then again, always open yourself to other possibilities and reconsider your first impression of other people. Refining in on your capability to analyze people instinctively don't essentially involve intense analysis. You have to be calm and open to what your instinct or gut feelings tell you and have the capability to reflect on what you hear and see.

Appearance

You are often able to tell a lot about someone's personality by just looking at his overall appearance. This is especially the case when you take your time to look at the smaller detail of how people dress and carry themselves. For example, the quality of clothes and fabrics used can reveal the person's level of income. A preference of whether they want casual or formal styles might say something about their personality. Jewelry, accessories, and tattoos may tell something about their hobbies, jobs, interests, and lifestyle.

Context and Environment

It's also very important to consider the environment and context you're observing someone's behavior in. If you see someone sitting in a meeting room with both of their arms crossed, it might indicate that the person is feeling defensive or they're just feeling cold. If you are trying to listen to people talking, do you think their answers are relevant to the topic being talked about and straight to the point? Or you think they are being too detailed and adding information that could have been cut off to shorten their answers?

Facial Characteristics

Another thing that tells a lot about someone's personality is their facial impression. But of course, the finer the details, the easier it would be for you. Check out whether someone has developed permanent frown lines on their forehead or the bridge of their nose from frowning too much. Maybe they developed wrinkles on their eyes because they laugh or smile too much? Do you notice them having pursed lips or clenched jaw, or their mouth is just relaxed? Do you notice their eyes were bright and glistening, sad, dull, or guarded? How easy it is for them to make eye contact?

Touching

The way someone touches other people and the way they touch you, if they do, also tells a lot of things about them. When you shake their hands, do their hands feel cold or warm? Firm or shaky? When they hug you, do they touch your back or just place their hands on the side?

8.2 Understanding Dark Psychology

Dark Psychology is a form of study on the human condition as it links to the people's psychological nature to prey on others driven by criminal or deviant initiatives that don't have many purposes as well as general norms of instinctual motivations as well social science theory. Anyone in the world, regardless of where they are from and what walk of life they are in, has this probability to abuse other humans and other living creatures. While a lot of people restrain this tendency, some simply carry out these impulses.

Dark Psychology is meant to recognize those feelings, thoughts, insights, and subjective processing systems that bring about destructive behavior that is adversative to modern understandings of human behavior. Dark Psychology thinks that criminal, different, and abusive actions are purposive and have some balanced, goal-oriented drive most of the time. And sometimes, Dark Psychology parts from the Teleology and Adlerian theory. Dark Psychology assumes that there's an area inside the human psyche that allows some people to commit terrible acts without any purpose. This theory has been labeled as the Dark Singularity.

Dark Psychology postulates that the entire humanity has a tank of malicious intent towards other people ranging from slightly conspicuous and transitory thoughts to pure psychopathic divergent behaviors which lack any unified rationality. This is what is known as the Dark Continuum. Justifying factors which acts as accelerants and approach the Dark Singularity, and where someone's atrocious actions fall on the Dark Continuum, this is where it is called the Dark Factor.

Short-term introductions to these concepts are explained further below. Dark Psychology is an idea this writer has coped with for 15 years. It has just been of late that he has lastly abstracted the philosophy definition and psychology of this feature of the human condition.

But Del Paulhus has jumped on the trend, with a series of studies probing into the Dark Side of human personality. As Paulhus notes in a paper published in *Current Directions in Psychological Science*:

"Our work on the "dark side" stands in stark contrast to the popular work on positive personality traits. In our view, dark personalities are more fascinating than shiny, happy folks."

Paulhus, along with his colleagues, has counted four different types of selfish and socially violent individuals who many of us deal with in our everyday lives: Machiavellians, Narcissists, Nonclinical Psychopaths, and Sadists. He says that psychologists usually confuse these types of people, who all share a propensity to score particularly high when it comes to lack of empathy. All of these kinds of people also tend to be sociable and extroverted, so they usually make a good first impression, before heading their way to make the life of other people a living hell. But then again, there are great differences, and those differences have important insinuations for the form of harm these people can do to the people around them.

He described Narcissists as *"grandiose self-promoters who continually crave attention."* He also says notes that Frank Sinatra was somewhat a narcissist, which was a trait many artists and celebrities, especially today, in the generation of social media carry.

According to Paulhus, *Machiavellians* are the master manipulators. There are the ones who have cheated us out of something valuable. And they are so good at it that we didn't even notice that they did it until it's too late. Unlike narcissists, they have soaring scores on tests of manipulativeness, and their disposition to be involved in white collar crime is just fairly high. The stock trickster Bernard Madoff, who made his way up to the New York Stock Exchange leadership and used his position to cheat his investors out of hundreds of millions, is a true-blue Machiavellian.

As Paulhus says, *Psychopaths* are "arguably the most malevolent," with high score when it comes to measures of impulsivity, callousness, manipulativeness, as well as grandiosity, which make them a dark force across the board. They usually do harm to other people as they tend to seek thrills without caring much who they will hurt along the way. Because they tend to be impulsive, they are less adept when it comes to white-collar crime in comparison to Bernie Madoff variety, and usually inclines them towards ferocity when other people try to get in their way. Whitey Bulger and Charles Manson are some of the people who had grave cases of psychopathy. However, Paulhus notes that there are a lot of individuals whose psychopathy is pretty low that it's not enough for them to be put in jail.

What is really troubling about this first set, however, is the fact that they are socially skilled and are able to make impressive impressions. For instance, compared to an average person, they are really good when it comes to interviews; this could be due to their high self-confidence and low anxiety level.

Everyday Sadists share the trait of callousness along with other types mentioned. However, the difference is that they are not impulsive or manipulative, but instead, they enjoy cruelty so much. As Paulhus says, this type of people might be drawn to jobs like the military or police officers, where they are able to have the chance to harm other people in a legal way. Paulhus isn't saying, parenthetically, that all people in law enforcement are sadistic; he's just saying that a lot of people in that industry carry that kind of personality.

By reading the paper released by Paulhus, I wouldn't be surprised if you get curious about this author – why on earth would anyone spend their time just to research on psychopathy, narcissism, and sadism? Does he carry the same traits? Well, not really!

Paulhus' interests on the dark side of personality rooted from that same scientific element formed in his mind. In the previous article he wrote on the dark side of the personality, he says that he got into this subject due to his concern regarding "*construct creep.*" He got worried about how many researchers who researched narcissism, for instance, did it without concurrently considering psychopathy or Machiavellianism, would begin to inflate the term to include the other related, but different, ideas.

For Paulhus, it is very important to differentiate the different types of dark personalities as there are real consequences people may face for lack of awareness – a person who is Machiavellian can do a different form of damage compared to the one who is psychopathic or narcissistic, for example. For the reason that these people share a propensity to do well in first interactions, Paulhus stressed that it's necessary that employers use great clean measures of those concepts as part of their personal valuation batteries. And based on what some of many people have told me, some people would have enjoyed having those measurements at hand before choosing their long-term partners.

CONCLUSION

What can you take from this book and how can you apply it?

I'd be lying if I told you that reading one book or a couple of articles would help you analyze someone's personality accurately. As you can tell from what's written in this book, it's a little bit more complicated than that. However, the good news is that with the right knowledge and awareness, this is something that is not impossible for anyone to learn.

If you read this book carefully, you'd know by now how to start. With the information written here and the exercises you can follow, you will be able to analyze someone in no time.

You must also always remember the most important but the trickiest part of the process – getting to know and truly understand yourself as a person. Find out what you really like, dislike, and what makes you tick. Once you fully understand yourself, then you have more than half of the battle won. While every person is different, we are also the same in many ways. After all, we are all people. All of us have the same basic needs.

All in all, you have to know that analyzing people is being able to recognize what's normal and what's not in human behavior. It's not really just about your ability to read someone's mind. Keep in mind that analyzing people is an innate process. Skilled analyzers of other people are known to have a great understanding of human personality traits and nature. They can easily distinguish different situations, and they know that context and time can highly impact one's behavior. They know the meaning behind certain different postures and body languages. Good listening and observation skills are crucial to be able to analyze other people! Equally important is the ability to trust your own perception and understand what you see, hear, and perceive about others.

Now, you can make the move and start analyzing the first person next to you. The moment you find yourself being able to analyze the personality of that person, you can take a step further and start doing it on the first stranger you see.

THE UNKNOWN SCIENCE OF

DARK PSYCHOLOGY

BY

KYLE MURPHY

INTRODUCTION

In a world where we are surrounded by darkness and troublesome people, we have become eager to learn why such people act in certain ways, and endure such a dark mentality. The secret to unlocking power and influence in society revolves around this topic. People who usually practice dark psychology do not often understand it, but for the few who do, will possess the power to get what they want in life in a malicious way, often leaving others powerless. This guide will help you understand and master many different aspects of dark psychology such as: The secrets of dark human behavior, the dark triad, emotional manipulation, hypnotism, NLP, dark seduction psychology, psychological warfare, deception, brainwashing, persuasion, and undetected mind control.

We are going to create light in this darkness by clearly elaborating on the hidden secrets of dark psychology. In case you are interested in knowing the techniques of dark psychology and their application, this book is all you need. Knowledge is always power, and people who access this information can make informed choices to do good or bad for themselves or someone else. You can choose to have the world at your fingertips the right way or the wrong way, as this book addresses both.

You are going to learn the dark art that can take you into the very depth of unexplored worlds, and go from virgin skin, to a master in disguise in just a matter of time. This guide is for the bold and macho who want to unleash their true potential and are tired of getting shackled back by a world of secrets. It is also for the weak minded to gain control and watch for the signs and gain insight on how you choose to live your life.

CHAPTER 1

WHAT IS DARK PSYCHOLOGY

Dark psychology is a human condition amongst people who prey on the misfortunate events of other people and their lives. Every human on this earth has the potential to victimize others, but many restrain the behavior to act on the impulse. These criminals know no emotion, have no remorse, and lack instinctual drives in social activity.

Dark Psychology Defined

Dark psychology assumes that all humanity has malicious intent toward others, ranging from mild to extreme. Extreme behavioral intentions consist of pure psychopathic thoughts and actions without any coherent ability to know otherwise. Mild behavioral intents include dark thoughts and plans that get pushed aside resulting in the person just being "normal" or a part of society.

Everyone has a dark side, and we are all capable of thinking and doing the worst—what others might classify as dark and evil. Dark psychology represents this fact as a mindset in humanity. Some people try to ignore it, and others embrace it. A dark human may believe and act "evil" because they want to gain power, money, sex, vengeance, or any other selfish purpose. Some people hurt others because it satisfies and pleases them, meaning, they commit horrible acts without objective and have no goal or determination to make them do so.

Dark psychology suggests that everyone has the potential to act brutally. This manner has access to our thoughts, feelings, and perceptions. As one would think or hope that these thoughts were nonexistent, the few people that embrace these thoughts act on them. This is called dark psychology—the few who act impulsively to their dark thoughts and use techniques against the ones who don't.

What Is a Dark Personality?

Someone that has a dark personality will have less empathy then others will. To define what being a dark character means is to develop traits that you would see in a sociopath. To have a dark temperament means to do intentional devilish things to someone or something. A person that consists of having a blackened persona will act and think in inhumane ways without thinking twice about it to gain satisfaction for themselves.

The more in-depth definition is "having developed traits or aspects of those like a narcissist, psychopath, and Machiavellian." This is known as the dark triad, which we will explain in the next chapter. Let's dive a little deeper and explore the signs of if someone were to have a dark personality:

❖ **Manipulation**

It means to skillfully master your words in making the victim do as you please without them knowing you are doing it. Flattery is an excellent way to manipulate someone. It means to boost someone's confidence and prey on their low self-esteem to get the victim to do as he or she pleases.

❖ **Moral Lacking**

They are unremorseful when they hurt you. They may say sorry, but only for you to believe they are sorry when they aren't, known as a strategy and technique they use to have you continue to be their victim. In addition to this, once you are down, they will further upset you by making unthoughtful cynical remarks.

Cynicism

They motivate by self-interest and skepticism. They do not trust that people are genuine and sincere. The dark person will show signs of achieving their selfish intents no matter the consequences and feel no obligation to fulfill their intentions in a mannerly way. This can also be classified as egoism.

❖ Narcissism

This means when people become all about themselves. They have an extremely high self-absorption and tend to need lots of attention. If not given the attention, they will succumb to malicious behavior and manipulating you into thinking it's your fault.

❖ Psychological Entitlement

This means they think they are better than others. They see themselves as more than someone else, and no one is equal. If they see that someone is or has better, they pinpoint them as their victim, and use "fake feelings" or whatever they need to do to knock their victim down a notch or two.

❖ Psychopathy

This happens when the person has lack of interest for others and is unaware of their feelings and the feelings of others. When they do something hurtful to their victim, they show no signs of empathy or desire to help. They lack self-control and react strictly on impulse.

❖ Sadism

This is a trait where the person finds it extremely satisfying to inflict pain on others. To inflict physical harm and emotional abuse on their victim gives a sadist the utmost pleasure and sometimes feel orgasmic to them.

❖ Spitefulness

This means that someone will do anything to retaliate against you even when you know you have done nothing wrong. They will go so far to retaliate or inflict torture to their victim that it may also hurt themselves.

People who consume these behaviors or show these signs are likely to have low self-esteem and cannot accept that other people are more successful than they are. They will show extreme signs of jealousy and do whatever they can in their power, to have what the victim has or to be better than the victim.

How Do People Develop a Dark Personality?

Whether we want to accept this aspect or not, it is a proven fact that all humans have the potential to be evil-minded. Well, this can stem from someone's past, or it can be nurtured into the way someone has grown up, such as previous life experiences they may have had.

As children, we often view the world and make our judgments based on our influences and way of life provided by our parents or guardians. If a child does not feel their superiors unconditionally love them, they will start to develop low self-esteem and lose confidence. Their perception of trust is defined, and they will continue to try harder and harder at gaining the love and attention they so desperately need. An example of this is when a child gets an A, and their superior asks if they can get an A+ next time. This shows the child that their A is not good enough and there is no reward for their behavior. As this continues to happen, the child may only feel worthwhile or loved in their parents' eyes when they are doing their best, and this creates a lifelong pattern of having to chase success while confusing success with happiness.

Another situation is if a child never feels good enough or is continuously compared to their siblings. The parent will pick a "favorite" child and devalue the rest. This household consists of having a parent who is already narcissistic and never thinks their children are good enough because of their self-deprecating values. A child who grows up with a narcissistic parent or superior tends to be more angry, defiant, and humiliated, thus resulting in adult narcissistic behaviors themselves.

Aside from this, there is no real explanation as to why or how someone develops a dark personality. It can be defined as having a rough childhood, being abused, hurt, and continuously let down, if you had a great childhood but got bullied in school, further resulting in hatred toward others and always protecting yourself and your family. Death can sometimes trigger a dark personality. Anything can trigger someone to become more ominous than they are as we all have dark attributes that we try to ignore. Anything can unleash the darker side in our-selves, and eventually, if someone were to get pushed far enough, they can develop their bad traits more dominantly. The fine line between good and bad is that some of us choose to embrace the bad and act upon those impulses whereas others choose not to, giving them more self-control.

Another thing to understand is that once someone gives into the dark side of themselves, they will start to realize that manipulation tactics work and will become addicted to the outcome of their newfound techniques. Once one understands that they can control the world around them to benefit themselves through many shady tactics, this is where the true development of dark personalities come from.

CHAPTER 2

THE DARK TRIAD

The dark triad is a term relating to the group of three distinct dark personality traits. These personalities include narcissism, Machiavellianism, and psychopathy. People that have high scores in these traits are more inclined to commit crimes, cause social distress, and create extreme problems for a company. People with these traits can use their techniques for selfish success such as being promoted in jobs like law enforcement, clinical psychology, and business management.

Narcissism is characterized by egotism, arrogance, and lack of empathy. Machiavellianism is characterized by manipulation, cynicism, lack of morals, and deception. Psychopathy is characterized by being antisocial, acting on impulse, being selfish, lacking remorse, and having little to no feeling, seeming insensitive to other people's opinions and themselves. The most common trait these personality types share on the "big five personality test" is low agreeableness.

What makes these personalities different from one another is that they each have a certain way about how they prefer to handle things. They each have behavioral and cognitive differences which make them all unique but similar. However, the dark triad traits are found to be genetic but have individual differences in the genes. Machiavellianism seems to be proven less genetic than the other two.

One thing you should understand about the dark-triad traits is that none of these characteristics can be changed in someone if they have it or show signs of having it. This is because it is part of their core personality, and sometimes the offender doesn't even know they are classified as being part of the dark triad group. These types of people can go on living life trying to feel an emotion and trying to be a part of society known as the "norm,". If you find yourself being any of these three, then it's down to you to change, which is going to take a lot of work and soul searching.

How to Identify Each Individual

Machiavellianism

The word comes from an Italian diplomat Niccolo Machiavelli, who wrote the book The Prince, which was interpreted as a certification of the dark arts of deceit. Traits of Machiavellianism include things like deviousness, manipulation tactics, self-seeking qualities, and lack of morality, and emotions. People who have high scores for this trait show high agreeableness and conscientiousness.

Machiavellianism is more popular in men than in women and is the true art of being unfair and cruel to others to get ahead. This stems from their lack of feelings and emotions for other people, causing them to struggle to grasp the aspect of empathy.

To recognize the signs or behavior of Machiavellianism, you must look for these things in someone:

These people will seem so focused on their own goals, ambitions, and interests that you don't seem to matter or faze them when you try to talk about yours. People with this trait will take power over the ones they love while at the same time they can come across as very charming and confident. When it is convenient for them, they will lie and deceive you to get what they want, and if you are the opposite gender, they will do so using flattery. Because of the lack of morality, empathy, and values in their life, they are a very dangerous group of citizens. It is detrimental to your mental health if you come across someone that seems too patient, has a history of casual relationships, doesn't take credit for their actions and find it difficult to interpret or handle their own emotions. They have a thick wall within their personality which causes it extremely hard to get to know them as well.

There is no known cure for this type of personality trait as with most people; for change to happen, you must be willing to accept you have a problem and be susceptible to help. Most people that have Machiavellianism don't even know that they have this trait, and often when they find out that they do, they won't accept it and go through life okay with who they are as they are very egotistical. Only a trained professional therapist that has experience in dark triad counseling can scratch the surface by using cognitive behavioral therapy. Unless it is court ordered or pressured to see a counselor for this trait, the person themselves are most likely not going to go as they also struggle in trusting and becoming close to people.

Narcissism

The word narcissism comes from a Greek hunter named Narcissus. He fell in love with his reflection whilst looking at himself in a pool of water which led him to drowned. Traits of this personality type can include being considerably selfish, conceited, arrogant, having no sense of compassion, and not taking kindly to criticism. People who score high in this trait show high numbers to extraversion and openness while scoring low in agreeableness.

It is important to know that you cannot change someone with this disorderly trait as their narrow-minded behavior will continue to repeat over and over again no matter what you do or don't do for them.

An example here would be, if someone's behavior in a relationship is that they are always demanding attention and trying to get you to admire them excessively. They often ask for too much, and when you cannot for fill their neediness they so desire, they will become hurtful and act superior to you thinking they are better while taking advantage of you in every way. They will express the exaggerated need to be reassured as they can create stories about you in their head so that whatever you do will never be good enough for their standards, thus leaving you wounded and mentally abused.

Another example of this you could be in the workplace, when someone may chat with their coworkers a lot, doing everything in their power to get to know them and impress them with their charm. As they need to feel superior, they gain their coworkers' trust by making promises (which they don't keep) becoming closer to them in a short amount of time. Once they become close, they will take credit for your work, and throw you under the bus without thinking twice about it. As an employer or a leader, they may single their employee they're victimizing out degrading those that are in a higher rank than them while having positive, great things to say to their face—being two-faced.

When dealing with a narcissistic character, a few things to watch out for are their words, emotions, and behaviors:

For words being used by someone who has narcissistic traits, watch out for words and sentences that lack compassion and interest. Once they think they have you and you aren't going anywhere, they will lose interest in you very quickly. If you decide to open up to them and show them your weaknesses, they will rarely take interest and be too quick to turn the conversation around on themselves. However, reversed when you point the blame to them, they will find ways to make you realize you are to blame and not them. If a narcissist gets turned down for a job or rejected by a girl, they will become overly obsessed with proving that they are better going out of their way to make the person who denied them feel bad. This is because of their egotistic nature and how superior they find themselves to be.

For emotions when dealing with someone with this trait, pay attention to how you feel when you're around them. If they seem too good to be true showering you with compliments and if you have a euphoric feeling when around them, this can be a warning sign. People who act in this way are not whom they may seem and will use their charm to get close to you as a way of winning rather than having and keeping. You are a game to them, nothing more as they will lack empathy for others' feelings. Later in a relationship, you may notice that you feel lesser than them as it is so automatic for them to build themselves up while tearing you down in the process. At first, you may not realize it. When a narcissist is in a group of people, they always seem to point the attention on themselves because they lack interest for what anyone else has to say. This is called "sucking up" all the oxygen in the room.

For behavior, pay attention to what they do over what they say. They tend to have distracting and convincing words to make up for their insensitive behavior. They rarely own up to what they have done and repoint the blame on you when you call them out on their behavior. They are very quick with their words finding every reason to defend themselves against you resulting in extreme communication problems. A great way to test their behavior is by asking them to do something like letting you know if they will be late coming home, and if they try to please and satisfy your request, then you may have nothing to worry about. However, if they don't then to end the relationship may be in the best for both of you as you cannot change the way this person behaves or acts.

It is good to remember a narcissistic person will never be blamed or take the blame upon themselves. It will always be yours or someone else's fault even for things they did to themselves. If they didn't get promoted, they would lash out at the closest person to them or their spouse's family as to point the blame on them. Nothing you do is ever going to be good enough as their expectations of you are always going to be just beyond your reach. They will humiliate children in public, sabotaging a coworker, or verbally attacking a friend or colleague. They will become obsessive to damaging relationships by angry venting on social media, creating arguments when there is nothing to fight about, or creating an atmosphere that is toxic for them and everyone around them. At the same time, when their relationship starts to fall apart, they will go back to flattery and charm to fix it as a "winning" technique. This is to keep their victim close, but at the same time not letting them get close enough to them.

Psychopathy

Personality traits associated with psychopathy include lack of feeling for compassion and remorse, antisocial behavior, and using techniques such as manipulation to get to people while being unpredictable in their actions. Take note that there is a difference between having psychopathic traits and being a complete psychopath. Psychopathy has been found to reflect all the "big five" personality factors making up who they are, agreeableness, conscientious, neuroticism, and openness leave the scale between the elements balanced. People who score high on the psychopathy scale show low levels of empathy and high levels of impulsivity and thrill-seeking behaviors.

Psychopathy is hard to spot in an individual because they can seem very ordinary on the outside while lacking compassion and a sense of right and wrong underneath the surface. They put on a charming mask. It works to become vindictive, volatile, and often (but not always) criminally inclined. It is important to note that a psychopath and a sociopath are different. A sociopath refers to a person being antisocial in association with environmental factors. A person with psychopathic traits is raised with violent surroundings causing their characteristics to be born with.

Psychopaths can understand and relate to people as they have no difficulty understanding what they think, want, or believe. Because of this understanding, they can further use their skills of deception and brainwashing to their advantage as they can pinpoint what the other person desires, using it to their advantage. However, this understanding is not automatic for them like most people. It is hard to determine whether someone has psychopathic traits because it seems the offender can switch the characteristics of psychopathy on and off. They can explain in full detail with no remorse or feeling how they managed to hurt, torture, or even kill someone, and at the same time understand how the person questioning them feels about it.

The differences between these three distinct personality types are they each have a different focus while at the same time all have the same goal which is putting themselves first to get whatever they want.

Machiavellianism manipulates others to gain personal skill, power, goals, or achievement. Narcissism believes they deserve all the attention and that they need to be treated differently than others as being unique or better. Psychopathy revolves around being insensitive to how they feel while still understanding the needs and wants of the people around them.

In conclusion to the traits identified by the dark triad, here is a summary on what to look out for in someone you may suspect might be any of the three:

- ❖ They manipulate others to extreme measures to get their own way.
- ❖ They compulsively lie to get their own way.
- ❖ They come off as charming or excessively flirt or compliment you.
- ❖ They exploit to get ahead.
- ❖ They lack sympathy, remorse, compassion, and empathy for others.
- ❖ They have a hard time being interested in morality views.
- ❖ They come off as insensitive, brutal, cruel, and spiteful.
- ❖ They seem to want affection or attention always and become clingy.
- ❖ They seek to be superior against others and often compare themselves.

The Dirty Dozen Test

The dirty dozen test consists of four studies and results in the testing for people with Machiavellianism, narcissism, and psychopathy. This test consists of ninety questions and items spread across three scales. This is called the "dirty dozen" test and determines the likelihood of the dark triad in people.

There are two reasons the dirty dozen test was created to measure the dark triad. First, each calculation has its unique response and limitations. Example, the Mach IV (measure to calculate Machiavellianism) is biased by social desirability. The Mach IV did not exceed .70 on the twenty-item scale, which is considered a low number. The NPI (narcissistic personality inventory) used to measure narcissism is composed of different questions which can be problematic.

Secondly, when studying the dark triad through a series of questions on the dirty dozen test, the screening also uses the "big five" identity test. The "big five" identity test comprises five principle identity characteristics making up an entire extraversion, neuroticism, receptiveness, conscience, and suitability. This test is a general sense of questions asking the student questions like on a scale of one to five would you strongly agree or strongly disagree. However, this test is very long and time-consuming, so the researchers of the dirty dozen testing used other measures and studies that are more efficient and time effective for both the researchers and the participants. There were four studies based around the dirty dozen in figuring out what traits resemble the dark triad.

To determine whether a participant is subjected to being a part of the dark triad, the dirty dozen (consisting of all three traits) will show results that are negative with agreeableness and positive with short-term mating and aggressiveness. Evidence proves that men score higher than women on all three of the dark triad traits. In two studies, researchers develop the calculations from the tests through principal components analyses (known as PCA's) and confirmatory factor analyses (also known as CFA's), also validating the dirty dozen through assessment of the nomological network.

In a third study, they test the consistency of over time process within a matter of 3 weeks as this can define the features of personality traits. Which also results in enough evidence claiming that the test and its usefulness is correct. Finally, in the fourth study, researchers refine their measure by simplifying a double-barreled item, improve the internal consistency of the scale, and again confirm the dark triad dirty dozen's factor structure.

Study 1

Researchers created twenty-two applicant items inspired by the original dark triad measures. Study one consisted of comparing and combining the dark triad traits with that of the "big five" and measures of mating results. The method was 273 psychology students composed of ninety men and 183 women between the ages of eighteen and forty-seven years old. Ten people at a time sat in a lab and completed surveys; once finished, they were thanked and sent off on their way.

By using the big five inventory, researchers were able to accurately assess the big five personality dimensions using a response scale from one to five. Narcissism was assessed with the forty-item NPI. The questions to determine an NPI were "I have a natural talent for influencing people" and "I am not good at influencing people." When the total number was summed up for narcissistic students, their score equaled to .80. Psychopathy was assessed with the thirty-one-item scale 111 (Roman numeral 3). The questions that were asked were, "I enjoy driving at high speeds," and, "I think I could beat a lie detector." The total number for psychopathy students equaled to .74. Machiavellianism was assessed by a twenty-item Mach IV. The questions that followed this screening were, "It's hard to get ahead without cutting corners here and there," and "People suffering from incurable illnesses should have the decision of being killed easily." The outcome to tell if an understudy was a Machiavellian equaled to .65.

When everything was said and done, the researchers totaled all three scales together to give the dark triad result score. To have a result they conducted a separate PCAs and internal consistency analyses for each calculation.

The next three studies followed a similar structure and method to study one and got almost identical results in how to tell if someone had traits consisting of the dark triad.

CHAPTER 3

THE POWER OF PERSUASION

No matter what we do or where we are in life, we are always being persuaded to do something, whether it's by our colleagues, friends, family, strangers, the media, or the government. It is done very discreetly, but it is happening to us every day. Some people are better at the art of persuasion than others making the world their playground, while others dive deep in emotional disappointment for their efforts.

This chapter will teach you the different techniques on persuasion and what is considered harmful or dark persuasion. What the differences are between the two using solid examples, and understanding how to use persuasion to get your way with others.

The Techniques of Persuasion

There are six different persuasion techniques: reciprocation, social proof, commitment and consistency, liking, authority, and scarcity. These techniques can be used for proper uses and negative uses. The good techniques of persuasion mean if you—the customer—benefits from whatever it is that the persuader—friend or foe—is trying to get you to do, buy, have, or explain something. Good persuasion means to have both parties benefit from whatever it is you or the other person is persuading. Dark persuasion consists of the fact that only one party or person benefits from the situation. The difference between persuasion and dark persuasion is the intent behind the effective tactics. So let's take a look at the six different types of persuasion:

    1. **Reciprocation**

When you are in a mall or shopping around Christmas or holiday seasons, you sometimes may find that a salesperson will reach out and offer you hand cream, perfume, or some other product that will grab your attention. If you are interested and give them attention, they will persuade you to buy some of this or some of that constantly asking for more.

As a natural human instinct, we want to give back to those who give to us. This is a form of cooperation between building relationship and other active types of bonds. When trying to persuade through reciprocation, you want to try to be positive and give useful positive information, resulting in a good experience.

2. Social Proof

A good example of social proof is to watch something funny, and then notice the laughter from the audience behind the scenes of shows (like The Big Bang Theory or Friends). Then try to re-watch the same episode, but this time with the silence of no laughter from the background crowd. You will realize the meant-to-be-funny parts are not all that funny anymore. According to recent facts, we will laugh longer and harder if the background crowds on shows are laughing too. This is called social proof.

If we see that others are doing something positive or negative, we are influenced by social evidence that what we are being persuaded to do is okay. Do you find in public situations something to you seems awkward or funny, but instead of reacting you will take a scan across the room to see if others noticed or feel the way you do? This is to ensure our reaction to the scenario is acceptable or "correct." People skilled in persuasion techniques will use this against customers like us because they know the frame of mind "if everyone else is doing it, or having it, I must too."

3. Commitment and Consistency

As we have grown into society, the media and the world around us make us know that common sense is to keep our word when we commit to something and we should consistently keep that behavior. This is being noble and honest. We don't like being called "wishy-washy" or indecisive, so we strive to commit and be consistent when it comes to this. If we don't then we may face and feel social shame being labeled as inconsistent.

Commitment and consistency persuasion techniques are used on people to "get their foot in the door." An example would be a business person or persuader will request something small of you, and then if you say yes, they will strike again asking for something bigger the next time. This is a way for the persuader to get to know your likes and dislikes so they can expect you to say yes again and again. Before you know it, you are committing to them through consistency and getting asked bigger and bigger requests that you can't say no to.

4. Liking

This technique consists of people that know what you like, based on previous tasks or orders you have done or made. We tend to say yes when we feel important to a company such as Avon or Scentsy. A typical sales technique is to make the customer feel special in such a way that they come back for more and more. Ever notice how when you stop buying things from these companies, they don't seem to notice you exist anymore? But then a few months down the road when you have forgotten about their company or business, you get an email or a phone call reminding you that you are still important to them and that they haven't seen you in a while. Then you are back in the triangle again becoming a valued customer. This is called the liking persuasion technique.

5. Authority

Here's some examples of authority persuasion: A friend may tell us that we might have a health problem, but we choose not to believe them, therefore we get rushed to hospital a few weeks later, and being told by the doctor that we have a health problem, leading us to be quick to believe what the doctor tells us. When we are young we get told that brushing our teeth will keep the dentist away, even though we still grow up forgetting to brush our teeth and after going to the dentist just to be told the same thing. But when we were young, we didn't believe our peers until we got older and trusted the authority. This is known as authority persuasion.

The fact of this is that the authorities have more knowledge in the field that they are in. Doctors and professionals have explicit knowledge in their professions that our friends and family members may not know much about, and therefore we will believe authorities over our close relationships even if they are proven right. It also gives us reassurance to point the blame when we get misinformed.

6. Scarcity

If you have ever watched an infomercial, you know their tactics sound a little like this: "This is a limited time offer. Call or subscribe now to get a discount or promo code." This is a tried and true technique persuader will use to get you to buy their product or request. When there is scarce resource surrounding their topic, this is when the person persuading you is in competition with other marketers because of the scarcity in the resources.

The idea behind this technique is to convince you that you are missing out on something and if you don't act immediately, you could be at a great loss. The persuader knows that people are motivated by the thought of losing something over the thought of gaining something for a better or equal value.

In conclusion to these techniques, it is essential that you understand the tactics used, as these six techniques can be used almost anywhere with just about anything. To understand persuasion, you first must put the facts together. The goal is to build honor, trust, and consistency upon your presence.

The Fine Line between Manipulation and Persuasion

As said before, dark persuasion is based on the use of its intent. Marketers and businesses will use persuasion techniques to help you understand why you must choose them whether their purpose is for good, where it will benefit both parties, or bad, where it will only benefit them. Now the same goes for manipulation. If someone were to use dark persuasion techniques, they are trying to manipulate you in some sort of way. Manipulation means to control or prey upon someone's misfortune to get what they want, which is the same tactics used for dark persuasion.

The real difference is based on three core aspects: the intent behind the desire to persuade someone, how accurate the process is, and the benefit or impact and the individual. Manipulation is to fool, control, or orchestrate the other person into doing something, buying something, or believing something that is false in a persuasive kind of way. This can leave the victim harmed or without benefit before they even know. Another way manipulation works is if the persuader moves their victim to the point of view that only benefits themselves. Now if the persuader doesn't use their persuasion skills correctly, then it leaves their victim less receptive to the idea because they will know that they aren't being benefitted.

Here is an example of manipulative, dark persuasion:

Say for instance i was selling a vehicle, I knew all about manipulation, and I had a plan to persuade my customer. This customer walked into my store and made it known that she had a family with four kids, the request was to look for a family-oriented vehicle. But instead of selling them a family-oriented vehicle, I persuaded my customer to buy a two-seater convertible by telling them that it would bring back their youth. I preceded to say that their kids would love her more because of the nice vehicle she has just bought. It would be teaching her kids to follow their youthful dreams no matter what. Meanwhile, I know that I would be making twice the commission on that car rather than a car that was more suitable for her. She drives off her stylish convertible, thinking she won the better deal, and here I am sitting here grinning from ear to ear, knowing the paycheck I am about to get because of that arrangement.

That's manipulation!

Now looking on the other scale of things, if that same person came to me and said they just wanted a stylish convertible, even knowing they had four kids, but they just wanted to blow some money. I could turn around knowing the same persuasion tactics I used in the first example but instead, I convinced the woman it was a better idea to buy the family-oriented vehicle because it would be in her best interest. I would lay out the facts, and at the end of the day, she drives off happy that she made the right decision about the family car.

This is persuasion not manipulation.

In the first example, I am using dark persuasion to benefit myself without my customer knowing. I will get a better paycheck, leadership skills in my job, and also i'd get bonus points with my boss. The customer, however drives away with the car they love but may have complications down the road with their family, having to buy another car. Because I don't care (having a lack of empathy) getting what I wanted out the deal (manipulation), I won't see this customer again, and so it doesn't matter (lack of morality). Let's say for instance she comes back to me and gets upset with me for convincing her to buy the vehicle she didn't want, I could just say, I suggested, and you bought it, this is not at all my fault, also taking no responsibility for my actions because this is the way I set things up from the start.

How to Persuade People

Now that we know the definition of persuasion and the difference between the good and bad techniques, we can further investigate how to persuade people ourselves. Whether you use it for good or bad will depend on the reason for why you are persuading to begin with.

There are three steps to persuading someone to do what you want. You must use effective communication skills, listen, and learn what the other wants and needs and then plan your moves. Let's look:

1. **Speak Effectively**
a) **Tell a good story.**

When we want someone to do something for us, we need to share personal or informative information to get them to relate. Start at the beginning and talk about the request at hand. Share how you arrived here by opening their minds to the experiences you have gone through, being careful to understand their feedback. Once they know what your story is, they will be more likely to share theirs. You just got an inside scoop to persuading them into what you want by containing more information about them.

b) **Use ethos (a speaker's credibility), pathos (emotional appeals), and logos (appeals to logic).**

When conversing with the person, you are trying to persuade—or manipulate—include in your story information about your credibility, provide a logical argument, and find their weaknesses to exploit. Tug on their emotional strings. Explaining your credentials will help them trust you, creating and mastering your bond. Once the bond is stable, talk about the logical reasoning behind your request still appealing to their interests. Once this stage is complete, you can further break out their weaknesses and get them emotionally invested by having them relate to your story backed by facts using the trust you have gained from them from the beginning.

c) **Prioritize your order of communication.**

One mistake a lot of persuaders make is sweet talking first. This will come off as beguiling, and your customer or victim will lose interest quickly. Instead, be straight up and forward with your request and ask for exactly what you want bluntly but respectively. After you have done this, put on the charm. The goal to this is making the customer feel they want to help you, rather than feeling like you must suck up for them to help you.

d) Don't ask them to decide right away.

As human nature, it is relevant that most people do not like to make decisions. When you ask them to make choices, they are more likely to think about it longer and come up with all the pros and cons which stalls time. The point is to ask for what you need and to convince them why it's a good idea to say yes. The last thing you want to do is cause them stress, so it is much easier to get someone to say yes rather than waiting for them to say no.

e) Speak positively and with confidence

People tend to respond to people with confidence and a sense that they know what their influencer is talking about. When you declare positive statements effectively, your customer will be more inclined to listen. Instead of saying, "Don't hesitate to call me," say, "Give me a call on Monday."

2. Listen Effectively

a) Start with small talk.

Make sure they are relaxed or in a comfortable environment. Ask them about their lives and engage with them. Create a casual atmosphere with the person you are trying to persuade by breaking the ice and having a friendly small chat. People are more willing to listen and do when they know you are wanting to become a friend first. When they tell you what they were thinking of doing, that gives you the open door to ask them more about their ideas, continually engaging with them to make them feel special and noticed.

b) Notice their body language.

Match your customer's body language to forge an emotional bond with them. Mirroring someone's body language tells them that you are like them and want and need the same things.

c) Listen more and speak less.

The more someone talks, the more you can understand their hopes, desires, and what they expect. This is crucial for a successful persuasion tactic. People enjoy talking more than listening, so if you give them the freedom to speak, then you can understand and plot more ways on how to persuade them for your benefit. Make sure to respond to their topic and ask questions; this shows them you are listening and can be trusted.

d) "Fill in the blanks."

When you ask someone a direct question, sometimes it may trigger feelings of being put on the spot. So use sentences to convince rather than a conversation filled with questions for them to choose. For example, instead of saying, "Would you like to buy a car?" say, "If you bought a car, I think you would feel…" and allow them to finish the sentence or end it with something positive and original.

e) Sway the conversation toward a more needs focused ideal.

By listening to them and following the previous steps, you should have a better understanding of what they need. Then once you've understood what they need, you can share some of your needs as well so that they can relate to you. When someone can relate to your needs, it will be easier for you to determine how they can help you or how you can help them, whichever way you decide to go.

3. Plan in Motion

a) Choose the right person.

The best person or victim to persuade is the person you are closest to and has the best emotional stability—someone that may need you as well as much as you need them.

b) Wait for the right time.

Choosing the right time like after lunch is usually best. People are more likely to listen and negotiate if they are not hungry. Most people get what's called "hangry"—this is when you are so hungry that you become irritable or grumpy. Hunger often causes things like anxiety, tension, and negative feelings so choosing the right time to persuade will make it easier to succeed.

c) Help to be helped.

A technique called reciprocity can build trust and close bonds. Set your plan to help the person first; in return, ask them a few days later for their help. As stated in the previous heading, people will be more susceptible to help you if you do something for them.

d) Choose the right situation

When people are persuaded to do something, their environment should be friendly yet business like. A coffee shop, restaurant, or private home will work wonders. The atmosphere is what will help you the most when trying to persuade someone for yours or their benefit.

e) Rehearse your speech.

Don't go into the conversation with someone blindly only to end up winging it. First, practice at home in the mirror keeping in mind it is good to make a good impression. You must come across as knowing what you are talking about. Someone who is focused and has all their facts in place are normally the type of people to listen to. Once you have it dialed down in the mirror, practice with someone you know and see if it works on them.

CHAPTER 4

UNDETECTABLE MIND CONTROL

Undetectable mind control is when someone controls your mind without you noticing or don't even realize. It can also be reversed if you are managing someone else's mind; while they don't even understand or notice, you are using undetected mind control. So what exactly is mind control? Mind control is when someone uses the ability of manipulation through persuasion techniques to take over their victims' sense of power such as the way they think, behave, feel, and decide. A way to enable this is through hypnosis. Undetected mind control is the deadliest kind of mind control there is.

When someone knows or has intuitive that they are mind-controlled, later that gives them a chance to object verbally, physically, and mentally. If the person does not detect that their mind is being monitored, then they won't have enough time to build walls or run from the subject in time. Two types of undetected mind control tactics are interpersonal interactions and the use of media. Because of the use of smartphones and laptops, we have some of the coldest walking manipulators on earth.

How to Tell if You Are Being Mind-Controlled

First, you must understand and learn all there is to know about mind control. If you know the signs, then you can further forego the steps to get away from it if you need. A big part of mind control is involuntary persuasion. As learned in the previous chapter, this is when someone manipulates you to do their bidding which puts you—the victim—under serious stress which can cause anxiety.

The second thing to look out for is a discreet control. A narcissist or personality of the dark triad will use trigger statements to control you. This is when they tell you of how they feel to get you upset or feel empathy for them, so they can remind you of how you are supposed to think, feel, and act.

At the start of this guide we mentioned about the dark triad and the traits that people have. Try and remember these and try to see if you notice any of these signs in your relationship or from a person you know, as you could be at risk of them being able to control your mind. These people have no empathy or emotion, so they will act selfishly and spin your words around to make you understand they aren't controlling you. If you feel isolated from others and think that if you were to leave them or live without them, it would leave you with nothing, then you have already been controlled, and it's a good time to get out while you can, and seek professional help.

These behaviors and techniques from the controller will leave you scared and filled with uncertainty that when you do finally escape, there is none. Or you feel there is no way out. If you try to explain to the authorities, they will look at it like you may be paranoid, and it isn't enough of a case to make, as from the outside it seems like you are in an argument.

However, there are ways you can escape. Reaching out for support through a therapist or a close relationship to you will help, and together you can brainstorm ideas of how to outsmart your victimizer. The process to escape doesn't happen overnight and will take time as there is no quick fix. Understand and accept that because of the way they have controlled you; you will consistently find it hard to trust yourself and others around you. The controller may have a hold on every person involved with your life so try to be discreet. Keep in mind that your self-esteem levels may have dropped, and your trust forms into paranoia, which may affect your decisions as if you feel your being watched all the time. Once you get out though, write what your experience was, how you felt, and what you went through so that the pattern doesn't repeat itself.

So let's rehash more simplistically. Here are five ways you can tell if someone is trying to control you.

Isolation

If the victimizer has you all to themselves with no one to turn to and almost nowhere to run, you're most likely under their control. A simple way they do this is by telling you that the new friend you made has something wrong with them and that you should be cautious. If you love them, then that is exactly what you will do, but some people get to the point of being so overly cautious that they would chase their new friend away, leaving them where they started with just their victimizer. The manipulator will do this to every relationship you have, persuading you to think there is no one you can trust but them because they have your best interest at heart.

Moody Behavior

If your partner seems childish and gets upset when they don't get their way, it can be one of the first sign's control is starting. If you are changing the way you act and think because you don't want to create an argument, then this is a for sure sign they already took your mind over. When you change the way you think, how you feel about certain things, and the way you act around this person or anywhere because of them, you are in the middle of a total controlling relationship. The way you were before you met this person is the way you should be, not having to change for anyone.

Meta-Communication

This is communication in which the victimizer gives you different body language than what they are actually saying. They have a hard time communicating their issue, and so they say nothing, clarifying that there is something wrong by their stand-offish behavior. This is a technique they use against you later. If this happens a lot and you ignore it, they can point the blame to you, saying that you don't care about them and that you should have known something wasn't right. Leaving you feeling you have to walk on "eggshells" later.

Neuro-linguistic Programming

NLP is a tactic manipulators use to layer thoughts using language into a person's unconscious mind without them even knowing about it. An example of this is, if a person is visually orientated, then the victimizer will use pictures and visual clues to plant messages inside the brain. If a person learns better by listening, then the victimizer will use secret auditory signals to get inside the mind without the victim being consciously aware of it.

Uncompromising Rules

Have you ever felt like your spouse set expectations too high or set you up for failure so you argue about it later? This is a form of undetected mind control. Some examples are, meet impossible deadlines like grabbing them a coffee when the store is twenty minutes away in five feet of snow, but they want it in ten minutes. Your life seems so structured that everything you do has to be planned out, and if there is one mistake, it's game over. Or when you don't know what will happen, but they need an explanation, and without reason, you pay serious consequences. What they are doing to you is taking your decisions and making you rethink, and doublethink everything you do so you follow a strict set of behaviors not to upset them. This is so you stop thinking for yourself and they can implant their agenda into your head.

If any of these techniques sound familiar or similar to you, then you should start thinking about ways to combat it or get out. As stated briefly before, people who do this stuff cannot be changed. They will change if they want to, and most times, they don't even know they are doing it because they wire their brains this way. There is no rationalizing with them, and there is no negotiating. You are in a vicious cycle, and it's your choice on what to do next.

How to Use Mind Control on People

So now we have learned how people can use mind control on us, let's flip the tables, and learn about how to use mind control on others. Again, just like the victimizer, learn the way people think, act and behave. Become an expert at analyzing people.

The first thing you need to do is to get to know your victim. Get inside their heads and understand their likes and dislikes. Know their world, who they talk to, what they do, what their schedule and routine is, what their hopes and dreams are, and their fears and failures. To do this, become attractive to them—become whoever your victim needs or wants you to be. This way it will make it easier for them to open up to you. The key to why you need to know the person is because when this person expresses a specific emotion, you can guess what actions he or she will take next. For example, if your boss or supervisor shouts or yells when they get angry but stops doing it when he feels shame or guilt, then making him feel guilty will force him to treat you better and strive to make you happy.

How to Use Emotions to Control People

Fear—when someone acts mighty to you, build up the confidence to act mightier than him, and he or she will shut down and not entertain the idea further.

Guilt—when someone gets angry or acts negatively but is affected by shame, then induce that it upsets you, and the person will back down.

Ego involvement—those that are arrogant and care about the way people look at them, tell them that everyone thinks you will not last, or that your friendship will fall apart if (Then state your Reason). Usually, this person will do everything in their power to make the problems better to preserve their reputation and ego.

Addiction—entice the person that has an addiction problem with whatever their addiction is, and they will bend under your thumb to get what they want, by pleasing you, as you become the source.

Anger—when an angry person yells at you or someone else, stand up to them with your anger. They will usually back down if your anger trumps theirs. It goes against the saying fighting fire with fire, but it can work to control their minds. They may think twice about being angry with you the next time.

By having an understanding of this person, you can see what emotion they have the most, in which you know which one to entice or induce more of. By doing this, it helps you gain control, forcing them to do as you want them to do by persuasion, brainwashing, or manipulation techniques.

How to Analyze Someone

To analyze means to study or examine something precisely and carefully methodologically. So when we analyze people, it is safe to say we are psychoanalyzing the individual. Psychiatrists and psychologists and professionals of the doctorate field will use this technique to understand further the way their mind works to create a successful treatment. To psychoanalyze someone, you must first let go of all preconceptions and judgment. You need to open your mind to understand the person in front of you fully. People who excel in reading, who are trained to see the invisible, and can read between the lines. There are three techniques to understanding how to read people.

First Technique: Observe Body Language Cues

It is a proven fact that words only make up 7 percent of how we communicate whereas body language and tone of voice make up the rest. Keep in mind not to try so hard to read body language, just sit back and silently observe.

Pay Attention to Appearance

Notice what they may be wearing. If they are buttoned up with shiny shoes, this indicates they may be ambitious people striving for success. If they choose a more casual look like jeans and a t-shirt, this may suggest a laid-back more casual personality. If they wear a tight top with quite a bit of cleavage, they may be the seductive type. Finally, if they are wearing a cross or Buddha pendant, this could indicate spiritual values.

Notice Their Posture

If they hold their head high, this could indicate they are confident. If they walk with their head down or slouch, this could mean they have low self-esteem. Maybe you might notice they arrogantly sway when they walk with a puffed chest. This could be a sign of someone who may have a big ego.

Watch for Physical Movements

When people lean toward something, it means they like that something, when they lean away, it means the opposite. If they cross their legs or arms, it can mean anger, defensiveness, or self-protection. Are they hiding their hands? This can say that they have a secret or could be hiding something. Lip biting and finger fidgeting mean they are uncomfortable and nervous, so it is a way to soothe themselves.

Look at Their Facial Expressions

You can tell a lot about a person's emotions through their facial expressions. A deep frown line indicates excessive worrier or an over-thinker. Crow's feet are joy smile lines. Pursed lips suggest anger, contempt, or bitterness. A clenched jaw signaled tension and built-up frustration.

Second Technique: Listen to Your Gut Instinct

Intuition is what your gut says, not your mind. It stems beyond logic and comes in the form of nonverbal feelings you perceive such as images and gut feelings. When reading someone, what counts the most is who the person is and feeling their aura rather than what they show you. Intuition helps you with this process

Honor Your Intuitive Instinct

In the first meeting, your gut will tell you how to perceive this person based on the first impression. This is an emotive reaction that occurs before you have the time to think. Are you at ease meeting this person or no? This is the trust meter that instinctually tells your brain what your take on this person is or should be.

Feel the Goose Bumps

Goosebumps are intuitive tingles that can either tell us that this person moves us or if they strike a nerve. They can also appear when you experience déjà vu a familiar feeling that you have known or been in this type of presence before, even if you have never met.

Pay Attention to Flashes of Insight

Be aware of the "aha" moments when conversing with someone. If you don't pay attention and take a mental note of this moment, you may miss it because of the rapid thoughts that go through your brain daily.

Notice Intuitive Empathy

When we relate to someone or connect with someone by a more profound meaning beyond explanation, we feel their physical symptoms and emotions. So when you are around someone you are trying to read, notice if you have pains that weren't there or feelings that came out of nowhere and only exist in their presence. This is also classified as sympathy pain.

Third Technique: Sense of Emotional Energy

There is a certain "vibe" each will give off. Similar to intuition, we can sense this vibe based on the emotional energy they portray. Some people give off a feel-good vibe of positive energy, while others may feel like you are suffocating in their presence. This discreet energy can be felt inches to feet away from you.

Sense People's Presence

This is the atmosphere that surrounds us, giving off the overall energy we emit caused by what makes us who we are—dark or light people, happy or sad. When reading people, notice if their presence seems friendly or attractive or if you feel chills up or down your spine making you want to run.

Pay Attention to People's Eyes

When we look into people's eyes, we can learn their energy. The body and the eyes have the same invisible signal telling us who this person portrays themselves as, or who they are. Someone's eyes can say a lot about them such as if they are caring, sexy, tranquil, mean, or angry. If their eyes are hard to read, this may be an indication that they are guarded.

Notice the Feel of Someone Shaking Your Hand or Giving You a Hug

When reaching out to shake someone's hand, notice if you feel warmth, comfortable or confident. Also, see if you want to pull your hand away as quickly as they touched you. What is the texture of their hand? Clammy, signaling nervousness and anxiety, or limp indicating being withdrawn or timid.

Listen to the Tone of Their Voice

While you listen to the person you are conversing with, notice how it makes you feel. Is their tone soft and soothing like your mother or elder, or is it short, snippy, or whiny? Based on these aspects of the sound in their voice, we can tell a lot about someone's emotions.

CHAPTER 5

Covert Emotional Manipulation

There are many types of manipulation, but the two we are going to discuss in this chapter are covert and psychological. Covert manipulation is when a person uses deceptive and dishonest tactics to change your way of thinking, behavior, and perceptions to gain power over you. Emotional manipulation consists of manipulating you when you are consciously aware, but not aware that the person is managing you. These two are the same. Someone who is skilled in manipulation skills will make sure your self-worth and mental well-being are in their hands.

Techniques of Manipulation

When a victimizer victimizes, their end goal is reflected by one thing, which is gaining power to benefit themselves. The manipulator will exploit in wicked ways, leaving the victim feeling mentally and emotionally exhausted. Some tactics go unnoticed for quite some time, and the damage is hard to fix when it has been done. Update yourself with the tactics so that you will be able to understand and pinpoint when it is happening. Here is a list of tricks manipulators use. It is important to remember this list may not mean that the victimizer is deliberately trying to manipulate you. They may not even know themselves that they are using these tricks.

1. **Home court advantage**

A manipulative individual may ask you to meet them in a private space such as an office, a home, a car, or other closed spaces. This is so they can exercise dominance and control.

2. **Let you communicate first**

A cop, salesperson, psychologist, judge, lawyer, and almost everyone in the work field will use the skill of getting you to talk first. This is so they can get inside your head and figure out your weaknesses, your hopes and dreams, ambitions, and fears. Once they know this information, it will be easier for them to exploit you and persuade you for their selfish purposes. They succeed at this by listening, observing, then asking you personal questions.

3. Manipulation of facts

They show very prominent characteristics. They will lie or make excuses for their behavior. They will make you feel guilty for their actions. They are often very good with their words withholding information on a need-to-know basis. Exaggeration and being one-sided is another indication of their manipulation traits.

4. Overwhelm you with statistics

When someone knows more of something than you do, they may make that well-known by throwing their intellect in your face. This is called "intellectual bullying," and they may only do this to feel smarter or better than you. In most cases, they will constantly overwhelm your mind with all the things you didn't know that they know. They will do this in front of people as to get a rise out of how you act. If you don't act, they have succeeded because this means their manipulation has gone unnoticed.

5. Overwhelm you with procedures and methods

Jobs, including law and political enforcement, use documents like paperwork, procedures, laws, and by-laws, committees, and others. This is to stall the victim and make them think their way is the way to think because they are correct. This type of behavior can stop a person from finding the truth, hide flaws, and avoid further examination. The government uses this to maintain power and control while keeping their position.

6. They may raise their voice

As a form of aggressive manipulation, some individuals may raise their voice. They believe that if they raise their voice and display negative emotions, you will become submissive to their compulsion and give them what they desire. Alongside the loud voice, they will use hostile body language such as towering over you and puffing their chest out.

7. Negative surprises

Negative surprises are surprises that put you off balance which lets them gain an emotional advantage. This can consist of low balling you in a negotiation situation, to a sudden task that the victim won't be able to complete or deliver. Usually, this comes without warning and may also result in requests as a means to continue victimizing you.

8. Give you little to no time to make decisions

This is a situation where the victimizer puts you under pressure by applying tension to control you. By doing this, it makes them hopeful that you will crack under pressure and give in to their demands.

9. Negative humor

Negative humor is when someone pokes fun at your weaknesses, making it seem like a joke so it doesn't become that big of a deal. In reaction to this, you may become angry and less secure. An example of this is, making fun of your appearance or intellect, what you have or don't have, making comparisons or bringing up your past and patterns. They do this because it will create a sense of emotional high standard control over you, leaving you humiliated.

10. Constantly judge you

Instead of humor, this is where the perpetrator bluntly makes fun of you and calls your weaknesses out; this is a form of bullying. They strive to make you believe you are not good enough and something must be wrong with you by picking out all your faults and exploiting them. No matter how hard you try, it never seems to be good enough because their expectations are too high leaving absolutely no room for failure. The offender creates a negative focus on you and your flaws without providing a solution to fix or offering any real means of help.

11. The silent treatment

The silent treatment is a good way for them to possess control over your mind, making you question and become uncertain. They do this on purpose to gain mastery manipulation as a type of head game. As you wait and become doubtful, they are on the other end, smiling at themselves, being proud that they have you squirming in your seat.

12. Pretend ignorance

Pretend ignorance is a "passive/aggressive" way to play dumb so that you will take on their responsibilities. This is a way for them to get you to do their "dirty work" so they don't have to. You will find this behavior in children who manipulate their parents into getting them to do their chores or something they don't want to do as procrastination. Some adults will do this as well if they have something to hide or responsibility they are avoiding.

13. Guilt-baiting

Guilt-baiting is a means of targeting the recipient's emotional weaknesses and opening their vulnerability to force them to do as they say or want. Guilt-baiting consists of irrational blame, pulling on heartstrings, and holding someone else responsible for their failure.

14. Victimhood

Victimhood is to play the "victim card" used to exploit the goodness and take advantage of good qualities in someone. They will pull from the recipient's guilty conscience, a sense of responsibility, and protective nature to get them to obtain selfish benefits. Some examples include exaggerated or made-up personal issues, health issues. Dependency and codependency. The manipulator plays weak and powerless to gain sympathy.

Characteristics of a Manipulator

The only reason a manipulator would be interested in you is if they can use you for their own personal gain. They will take what you say and do and twist it around so that you are left confused and unable to recognize yourself. Distorting the truth and lying are the two most significant factors that they will excel at.

The following are five characteristics of a manipulator. This list is provided so that you know and understand what to look for in someone, helping you stay alert and hopefully prevent you from getting pulled into their trap.

1. Selfish

Either they lack insight on how to engage with others or they honestly believe that their way is the only way. When their needs are being met, that is all they care about. Every situation that revolves their world is about them, not caring what others think, feel, and want.

2. No sense of personal space

When it comes to boundaries, offenders do not have them, nor do they respect others. If they get what they want, they don't think about who it hurts. They will crowd your space physically, emotionally, mentally and spiritually and be un-interested of how it affects you. It's like a parasite; they will feed off someone to leave that person to feel exhausted, weakened, and humiliated.

3. A good people reader

A perpetrator will look at their victim and be able to know if they have a good chance at trapping them. They prey on people's sensibilities and conscientiousness. If you are a kind, caring, gentle person, you are at risk of becoming manipulated. A manipulator will spot these good traits in you, and use your personality against you. They become what you need of them first, then they put on the charm until they have you. Then over time leave you broke and confused because they are getting or have gotten what they want from you.

4. Good conversationalists

The way the offender talks about others is more than likely how they are talking about you. They have mastered "triangulation" being where they create scenarios and dynamics that set up for hatred and jealousy while encouraging alienation.

5. They are not who they pretend to be

If a person tried to be good, they would be good. If a person decides to be evil, they will develop negative traits. Usually, what you see is what you get. So if someone were to be deceiving and untrustworthy, that means that is who they are portraying to be. If someone were to be kind and giving that is who they choose to be. If your offender seems too good to be true, it's because they usually are, so listening to your instincts is wise when you get this feeling.

How to Outsmart a Manipulator

We have gone over how to spot a manipulator and what their characteristics and techniques might be, but how do we outsmart them? If you are up against a manipulator, then there is something you may want to keep in mind when dealing with one. Here are some tricks to try.

1. The first thing to do is to avoid the offender. The first sign of techniques or tactics being used on you, divert their energy and run. If you have to make excuses why you can't hang

out, do that. If you need to say you are busy, then stick to it. The first and most efficient way to deal with them is to avoid them.

2. Learn to say no. Once you understand the meaning of no and take a stand for yourself so that you don't get pushed around, you will find that life is much easier to live. If saying no makes you feel guilty and you find this causes you to be afraid to say no to people, then this will only set yourself up to be taken for granted. Which is what a manipulator wants and looks for.

3. Ignore the offender. Ghost them. Walk away from them. Do whatever you need to do if you can't avoid them. This is just another form of avoidance, but if you can't walk away, run away, or say no, then ignoring them is your best bet. If you are around one and cannot get away, then nodding, pretending to listen with an "mhm" now and then is best.

4. Set boundaries. This may be the most important one of them all. At the beginning of any relationship you make, make sure you are very clear about what you will accept and what you want. Make it clear that you will and won't do or tolerate certain things. Whenever you say no or set boundaries, make sure you also add why this is acceptable or unacceptable, that way no misunderstanding takes place. It also shows confidence that you are a healthy individual who knows what they want and doesn't want.

5. Set goals. When you know what you want, who you want to be, and how you want to get there, it makes it harder for a manipulator to come in and take it from you. You don't have to know the answers right now but setting goals toward your future and for yourself shows that you at least want to try.

6. Get to know someone before you get emotionally invested with that someone. Once you can know for sure that they aren't out to get you, then you can remember to put your trust in them and build a life or friendship based on truth and facts. This isn't easy, and it takes some time to get to know someone—give or take six months to a year.

7. Become someone that they wouldn't want to mess with. At first, put up your walls and create this persona that what you say and do match up. You need to make your personality

prominent in the first couple minutes of meeting someone. Making your first impression a bold one will show a manipulator that you are not the right person to target.

8. Make others aware of this person and your suspicions. Do it discreetly so that you don't get burned in the end, but definitely strive to help others avoid this person. Make sure you have your facts right though, because if you are wrong, then you can really hurt someone's ego and life. You wouldn't want to make a false accusation then destroy their resources so they are left with nothing. The goal is to take their power away, not their life.

CHAPTER 6

BRAINWASHING

Brainwashing—which is otherwise known by many as mind control, menticide, coercive influence, thought control, thought change and reinstruction—is the idea that suggests that the personality of a human can be either adjusted or constrained by a bunch of mental strategies. Brainwashing is known to work toward reducing your ability to think on your own, to introduce new thoughts and ideas into your mind with the aim of changing your frame of mind, qualities, and beliefs. In brain science, the study of brainwashing, known as thought change, falls into the circle of social impact. Social impact is known as the way people can change the way in which they view life, their convictions, and practices.

For example, there is a technique that works to change a person's behavior who isn't worried about their frame of mind or morals. The training technique, which is also known as the "purposeful publicity strategy," occurs when you don't care about what's being taught and try to change a person's mindset, along with the lines of "Do it since you know it's the correct activity." Brainwashing has a serious type of social impact that combines different ways to deal with changes in somebody's state of mind without the individual's consent. Since brainwashing is such an intrusive practice, it requires the total loyalty of the subject, which is the reason you hear about the brainwash practices happening in jail camps or total factions.

How Brainwashing Works

The brainwasher must have unlimited authority over the objective or person being brainwashed with the goal of controlling the sleep routine, eating, using the washroom and the satisfaction of all other essential human needs rely upon the specialist. In the mentally conditioning procedure, the operator efficiently separates the subject's personality to the point that it doesn't work any longer. The brainwasher replaces it with another list of activities, morals, and ideas that work in the objective's present condition.

While most clinicians trust that mentally programming an individual is conceivable under the correct conditions, some consider it to be far-fetched or possibly as a less extreme type of impact than the media depicts it to be. A few meanings of brainwashing require the danger of physical damage, and under these definitions, most groups don't brainwash since they usually don't physically abuse people. Different definitions depend on "nonphysical compulsion and control" as similar methods for brainwashing. Notwithstanding which definition you use, numerous specialists trust that even under perfect conditions, the injured individual's old personality isn't killed by the procedure. However, it is secluded from everything, and once the "new character" quits being strong, the individual's old temperaments and beliefs will return.

Brainwashing steps and methods for

In the past, it has been established that a multistep procedure that has been developed, which starts with assaults on the detainee's feeling of self and ends with what seems, by all accounts, to be a change in the mindset of the person. Scientists eventually characterized a lot of steps associated with mental conditioning and brainwashing, such as:

- ❖ Strike on character
- ❖ Blame
- ❖ Self-treachery
- ❖ Limit
- ❖ Tolerance
- ❖ Impulse to admit
- ❖ Diverting of blame
- ❖ Discharging of blame

- ❖ Advancement and amicability
- ❖ Admission and resurrection

Each of these stages happens in a domain of segregation, which means all "ordinary" social reference focuses are inaccessible, and methods like lack of sleep and ailing health are regularly part of the procedure. There is the risk of physical harm, which adds to the brainwashing.

- ❖ Separation of Personality

This involves an attack on the personality of the subject, which includes ideas like, "You are not who you think you are," a deliberate assault on the character or inner self of the subject and his entire mindset. The operator denies everything that makes the identity of the subject, with statements like, "You are not a warrior," "You are not a man," and, "You are not guarding opportunity." The objective is under consistent assault for quite a long time, weeks or months, to the point that he ends up weak, confused and a shadow of himself. Thus his convictions appear to be less strong.

- ❖ Blame

You are awful. While the character emergency is setting in, the operator makes a feeling of blame in the objective. He savagely assaults the subject for any "wrongdoing." He may pick on you for everything from the "poorness" of your mindset to the manner in which you eat. You then start to feel a general feeling of insecurity.

- ❖ Self-selling out

When the subject is drowning in pitiful blame, the specialist drives him either with the danger of physical damage or of continuation of the psychological assault to hate his family and friends. This selling out of his morals and belief of individuals he feels a feeling of dedication to expanding the disgrace and loss of personality.

❖ Limit

Who am I, where am I, and what am I expected to do? With his character in an emergency, going through so much disgrace and having sold out what he has dependably had confidence in, the objective may experience what in layman terms is called a "mental meltdown." In brain research, "mental meltdown" is only a gathering of events that can show any number of mental changes. It might include wild crying, great sadness, and general confusion. The objective may have lost his grasp on the real world and have the feeling of being lost and alone. At the point when the objective achieves his limit, his feeling of self is ruined—he has no control over the identity or what's going on. Now, the operator sets up the compulsion to change over to another mindset that will spare the objective from his sadness.

❖ Leniency

Focusing on a condition of emergency, the brainwasher offers some kindness or relief from the mental torture. He may offer the objective a beverage of water, or pause for a minute to ask the objective what he misses about home. In a condition of breakdown coming about because of repeated mental assault, the objective may encounter a positive feeling and appreciation different from what he's used to, as though the operator has spared his life.

❖ An impulse to admission

For the first stage of brainwashing, the objective is confronted with the difference between the blame and torment of the personality strike and the sudden show of mercy. The objective may feel a longing to respond to the affection offered to him, and the brainwasher may introduce the idea of admitting fault as a way to removing blame and agony.

Diverting of blame

After long periods of mental breakdown, the objective's blame has lost all significance—he doesn't know what he has done wrong, he realizes he is not right. This makes something of a clean slate that gives the operator a chance to fill in the spaces: He can coerce that feeling of "misleading quality," to anything he desires. The specialist joins the objective's blame to the mindset the operator is attempting to create. The subject comes to trust that it is his mindset that is the reason for his sadness. The complexity among the old and new mentality has been built up: The old mindset is related with mental and physical misery, and the new mindset is related with the likelihood of getting away from the sad mentality.

- Discharging of blame

The troubled target is made to realize that there is a reason for his "bad mindset," that it isn't he himself—this suggests that he can get away from his situation by making a change to the wrong mindset. He is faced with the idea that should simply get rid of the general concepts and behaviors that are related to that particular mindset, and he won't be in pains any longer. The objective can get rid of the sad feeling by admitting to acts related to his old mindset and behavior. With his full acceptance, the objective has finished mentally dismissing his old mindset and actions. It is then up to the specialist to offer a new mindset and behavior to the target.

Conclusion

A procedure of brainwashing like we have just discussed, has not been tried in a research center setting, since it's harming to the objective and would be a wrong exercise. Scientists made these conclusions from direct records of the strategies used by people who brainwashed in the past and different examples of "mental programming" around a similar time. Since different scientists have distinguished mental breakdown from what seems, to be a group of steps that result in a new mindset, which is the reason a few people end up being brainwashed and others don't.

How You Can be Brainwashed

If you have ever watched the film "The Manchurian Candidate," you will see that a successful senator was captured by Korean soldiers and then brainwashed into becoming a sleeper agent for them. The intent behind the brainwashing techniques the Koreans used, was to assassinate the presidential candidate. The film clearly shows that even a successful man can be brainwashed, but in reality, the opposite is more likely to happen.

People that are vulnerable or have low self-esteem are the ones that are more at risk to be brainwashed. These types of people have lost a loved one to death or divorce, been terminated from their job, been forced to homelessness, or have a disorder or an illness that they struggle to accept.

A person who wants to brainwash you, will generally look for your strengths and weaknesses, figure out who you trust and who listens to you. This information is needed to manipulate your beliefs. The brainwashing process starts and takes five steps to do so:

1. Isolation

People who have friends and family are dangerous to the predator because friends and family can question their motives, therefore helping the victim to think. Isolation starts where the offender gets you to love them or create some sort of close bond with them so that you trust them. Once the trust and the relationship are made, over time they start making you question the influences around you. Once this process is complete, the perpetrator will then work on your influences getting them to turn against you after knowing your secrets. Alas, you are isolated without even knowing it. This can take up to a couple of months

2. Self-esteem attacks

When you are in a vulnerable state and feel like no one else cares, the subject hurting you will make a move towards your esteem. If you already have low self-esteem, it becomes easier for them to attack you. The ways they do this is to cause you stress so that you are not able to sleep, then enforce violence and abuse, intimidation, and embarrassment. Eventually, your life will be so controlled, you won't know when a good time is to sleep, eat or even use the washroom.

3. You vs. Them

A brainwasher will break you down so that they can address a better situation than the one you are currently in. By nature, humans are tribal and want to be part of a group. We are social creatures. When the brainwasher puts us in a dynamic group where we can relate to others that are brainwashed, the offender gains more control of you and your environment making you believe it is better where you are then where you were.

4. Blindly listening to them

The end result for a brainwasher is to have you look to them without thinking. Without you noticing, they want you to understand and relate to what they tell you or convince you to do. To achieve this goal, they will generally reward you with positive feedback or things when you listen. However, they will also reverse the effect and use negative punishment for when you don't listen to them.

Another way they can get to you is to chant or say the same thing over and over again. Repetitive phrases are a way to calm the brain, and it is proven that the analytical and repetitive parts of the brain are interchangeable.

5. Testing

A perpetrator will test their subject by committing a criminal act of some kind to see what their victim does or will do. If their victim seems fine and is programmed the way they left them, their test is working. When their analysis is shown positive, it tells them that the subject is still brainwashed, and lets the offender know they still have all control. There is a possibility, however, that the victim can regain their consciousness back and start thinking for themselves, hence, why the tests are in place.

To stop yourself from being brainwashed, you must live by a few rules.

- ❖ Don't believe into what you read.
- ❖ Don't let scare tactics phase you
- ❖ Pay attention to subliminal messages
- ❖ Be a leader and think for yourself
- ❖ Do not put yourself in a compromisable situation.
- ❖ Do your research
- ❖ Be unique
- ❖ Don't let yourself be isolated.

Help your friends and let other people be aware. If they are being brainwashed, get them out and support them through the withdrawals of the perpetrator.

Dark Psychology and Brainwashing

Dark psychology strategies are used by individuals around us consistently to control, pressure, and impact us to get what they need. Dark psychology is essentially the art and craft of the study of brainwashing and mind control. While Psychology on its own is the study of human conduct and has proven to be vital to our lifestyles, mindsets, activities, and behavior, the term dark psychology is the marvel by which individuals use strategies of inspiration, influence, control, and intimidation to get what they need. As indicated by most specialists, the study related to the term brainwashing occurs in different stages. The idea of mental breakdown and brainwashing involves different robust methods and types of psychological and physical pressure. The subject is quite often in a withdrawn area or a learning area which is usually far from friends and family, where they are around other subjects. The lack of sleep is very typical, as the change in eating regimen and example of dress code and behavioral patterns. Open self-blame is commonly supported under self-investigation. The subject's time is cautiously controlled and loaded up with a vast number of exercises. This backing can appear as addresses, readings, and other gathering exercises. This stage can be as short as a couple of days and can sometimes stretch out for a considerable length of time. It is intended to inspire such feelings as dread, blame, fatigue, and confusion concerning the enlisted.

This initial stage dives deeply into the second phase of mental breakdown in which the subject is urged to "experiment with" different exercises. These exercises may include such things as self-investigation, addresses, asking, and working at gathering related tasks. Such components might instill this act of cooperation as social weight, good manners, authentic interest, or a longing to gain support with power figures. This coordinated effort drives the subject to start to consider the intelligence of the mindset being referred to truly, this gives room to the third phase of brainwashing in which the real change in mindset begins. In this third stage, the subject usually affects the mindset, along these lines creating an especially powerful dependency on friendship. Furthermore, the information given to the subjects is cautiously screened to support the gathering lessons. The subject remains physically and emotionally weak, and this makes it troublesome for the subject to make any personal complaints about the whole process.

In the last phase of influence, starting mindset concerning the gathering and its idea is strengthened to the point that the newcomer comes to acknowledge the lessons and choices that have been instilled while seeing any other purpose that points to the opposite as being very wrong. By this point, the subject has been coaxed into taking a series of open as well as irreversible activities in support of the brainwashing. These exercises involve stress, mental breakdown, and a change in the mindset after some time. As an example, when the Symbionese Liberation Army was influencing Patricia Hearst, she at first was asked to prepare with the gathering. At that point, she was requested to copy a prewritten radio discourse. Next, she was asked to both compose and record such a discussion. She was required to go with the gathering on a bank burglary with an emptied weapon. The level of the behavior that was expected from her kept increasing over time with the gathering.

In this last stage, subjects stay surrounded by the people who carry out the teaching and brainwashing. These people verify the subject's impression of the rules and exercises. Also, they examine and record the subjects change in mindset and total identity change. As per late news reports, these techniques compare near those followed in the preparation of people involved in suicide bombings on planes once they express an underlying readiness to make such a change in their identity. Such people are guarded and confined in houses, lose access to family members, and frequently recordings are made to be used in future publicity endeavors. Specialists take note of that the strategies or stages that are portrayed in the past subheadings arrange a list of strong brainwashing systems and methods. Friend weight is known to be especially powerful when an individual faces a problem.

Individuals' capacity to oppose an idea is especially weakened when they do not have the chance to contemplate the idea because of dread, lack of sleep, and additional overactivity. When like-minded people such as those found in some gatherings talk about a point they happen to agree upon, the outcome is a common mentality, with gathering individuals taking a common conclusion after talking. Essentially, outrageous mentalities also occur when people find out that others share and appreciate their ideas. When people agree to severe and open punishment, they need to support such activities by using any mindset that helps these convictions, a procedure referred to as the "decrease of subjective disharmony." The aims of numerous fanatic gatherings dwell on the human need to feel essential, critical, and part of a social circle, whether it's a religious, political, logical, or notable group. In this passionate setting, the extreme influence related to the term brainwashing is a group of methods that, can inspire amazing changes in both the mindset and behavior of the subjects.

CHAPTER 7

NEURO-LINGUISTIC PROGRAMMING: THE BASICS

Neuro-linguistic programming is a lot of different aptitudes that communicates with the inner-self. It is a type of communication that consists without speech. To break it up, so it is easier to understand, let's take a look at the individual aspects of the word.

Neuro. This term refers to the mind and brain. It controls the state of mind that affects communication and behavior.

Linguistic. This term refers to the way our mind and body reacts to our language and nonverbal communication. Speech and verbal communication are tools we use to gain insights into the way our brain works, whereas neuro-linguistic programming language teaches us how to access unconscious information.

Programming. This term relates to the volume of the brain that controls the way we change our mind and body state. Programming refers to what you do subconsciously such as your habitual patterns and thoughts, feelings, reactions, beliefs, and traditions. Someone trained in NLP can access this part of the brain by accessing it through conversation so that outdated programmed behaviors can be changed.

So in short, neuro refers to neurology, linguistic relates to language, and programming refers to how both neuro and linguistic come together to make language functions work.

How Does NLP Work

The human language revolving around words makes up only 7 percent of meaningful communication. When someone says something, and then their body language and facial expressions say the opposite, that makes up 93 percent of the communication we use nonverbally. Someone's mindset, attitude, and feelings is an active form of communication. In the world of communication, a whole different way of interacting consists in your mind and through our body language.

Techniques Surrounding NLP

The techniques that follow are powerful and effective when changing how someone experiences and thinks about the world. NLP can transform someone's life since our thoughts and feelings shape our reality. These are the four most impactful techniques that are used:

1. Dissociation

Feelings of shyness, nervousness, and sadness, in some situations are automatic or unstoppable. Whether you want to build up the nerves to talk to that person you have a crush on, or if you have to get in front of a crowd and speak publicly. These situations bring on automatic, uncontrollable feelings inside us. Dissociation can help immensely with these automatic feelings.

a) Identify the emotion that you want to get rid of.

b) Imagine you are of an out-of-body experience, and you can look at yourself. Watch yourself from an observer's perspective.

c) Once this is complete, notice how you feel at that moment. It will change dramatically.

d) If you would like to go one step further, take yourself out of the body that is observing yourself, so you are looking at yourself watch your other self.

2. Content reframing

Reframing means to take a negative situation and make you feel superior by changing the meaning of the situation into something positive. A good example is this: You just ended a bad relationship. You are most likely feeling awful and sad which will be an automatic feeling an in human nature to feel. But by reframing the meaning behind the ending of the relationship, we can ask ourselves "what are the benefits of being single?" Say that you have learned valuable lessons from the previous link and now more doors have opened up to you. Like being free to do what you want, when you want, and you don't have to answer to anyone or have obligations to anyone but yourself. In short, reframing your mind to see a situation differently will give you a positive outlook on your experiences.

3. Anchoring

Anchoring is when you are conditioned to a particular response. Ivan Pavlov experimented with dogs to get this response. He would ring a bell repeatedly while dogs ate, after doing this a bunch of times, the sound made the dogs salivate. Once this happened, even if there were no food, whenever Ivan rang the bell, the dogs would salivate. This is an example of anchoring by creating a conditioned response.

You can accomplish this with yourself if you create emotion with a sound or gesture. As long as you can associate one thing (behavior) with another (thought), then you are anchoring yourself. Do this repeatedly, and every time you do that one thing you associate bad, you can do the other thing that makes your brain positive about it.

4. Getting other people to like you—rapport

This technique consists of silently and discreetly mirroring someone else's body language, tone of voice, and words. We like and get along with people we can relate to. If we imitate other people's actions, our brain sends pleasure sensors which make people feel a sense of liking to anyone who reflects them.

CHAPTER 8

THE FINE ART OF DECEPTION

Deception is the act of wrongly advising somebody about the truth of something. Imagine setting off to the doctor for a drug to help with a health concern, and for a while, you take your endorsed medicine to find later that you've been given a fake drug or sugar pill and were not treated for the sickness. Odds are, you will feel furious and baffled because of this trickiness. You may even think that your doctor acted wrongly.

In psychology, deception is far from being a true moral issue. A few doctors and specialists believe that misdirecting somebody who is part of an examination is deceptive and can make people feel clueless concerning the real idea of the test. Others trust that deception is essential since it keeps members from carrying on unnaturally; it is vital that members act in their true manner when they are not being watched or examined.

Indeed, even the most truthful people practice deception, with different examinations demonstrating that the average individual lies a few times each day. A portion of those untruths are huge, yet more frequently, they are seen to be harmless, comments like "That dress looks fine" are sent to maintain a distance from awkward circumstances.

While misleading oneself is commonly seen as hurtful, a few specialists maintain that there are specific sorts of self-deceit—like trusting that you can achieve an aim objective regardless of what might be expected—that can positively affect success.

Analysts have since, hunted down approaches to completely recognize when somebody is lying. A standout amongst the most notable, the polygraph test, has been questionable, and there is some proof that maintains people who suffer from specific mental issues like antisocial personality disorder can't be estimated by polygraphs or other frequently used lie recognition techniques.

Why We Lie

Nobody likes being fooled, and when open figures are caught in a lie, it can turn into an outrage. In any case, while a lot of people pride themselves on their trustworthiness—and try their best to avoid liars, we all need to come to terms with the fact that everybody lies, for a lot of reasons. A few specialists propose that a specific amount of deception might be vital for keeping up a sound working society.

How to Spot a Liar

Being able to spot a liar is a trick that many people feel they have. Few people can boast this ability. Take an example as, if you're talking to somebody you just met, who says that he knows one of your friends, however, this doesn't exactly seem to be accurate for you. It is possible that this person needs something out of you, to get the information that could be used against you. You're naturally hesitant to say anything, but deep down, you know it's possible for this person to know your buddy truly, and here comes your dilemma.

A lot of people are just not great at spotting deception. People usually watch out for signs that will help to spot a liar. However, liars show little or no symptoms that would imply they are telling lies. It's possible that sometimes, people may not be right in their suspicions about liars, but rather, the signs that are supposed to show when somebody is lying are just not reliable. There is also an idea that outward looks may give more signals than the liar's words or actions.

The key to spotting distinguishing deception is entangled by the way that making a decision about apparent versus presented signs isn't equivalent to deciding if an individual's facial expressions is that of someone that is lying or not.

Negative statements turn out to be a test since liars are not great at deliberately appearing to be angry. Specialists call attention to the fact that liars are less productive in faking negative feelings.

Notwithstanding these troubles, specialists trust that people could turn out to be right while recognizing the statement of liars whenever given the correct directions. A survey looked into two methods with regards to deception. In the first of two investigations, undergrad members saw recordings of individuals who were lying or coming clean, viewing these with no sound. The records were made by asking the performing artists to either lie or come clean about the manner in which they were feeling in the wake of having watched a film section of either The Jungle Book (positive emotions) or Sophie's Choice (negative feelings). The members viewing the recordings at that point gave their opinions on who they thought was lying or being truthful. As anticipated, members were not able to make accurate conclusions. When it came to rating the degree of the depicted feeling, members were more exact in rating negative than positive, passionate appearances. This discovery stresses the possibility that it is more natural for people to lie about a negative feeling.

The second examination included a more significant number of members, more video parts, and a more extensive arrangement of passionate expressions from the recorded appearances. The negative feelings scale included things that the creators accepted would be significant to trickery, such as lament, blame, misery, outrage, and stress. These discoveries affirmed those of the main examination, demonstrating that members couldn't tell whether the general population in the recordings were lying or not, but instead could rate whether the general population in the tapes were feeling happy or angry.

In representing this impact, the creators come back to the possibility that maybe individuals are not precisely great at spotting a lie when it includes a negative feeling. It is likewise conceivable, however, that eyewitnesses changed their mindset when they're seeing the feelings of somebody who appears to be sad, hurt, or sorry. It's notable that individuals are better at making subjective decisions when they're in a terrible state of mind. When seeing somebody who appears to be miserable, compassion sets in, and you feel awful too. By then, you'll be ready to pass judgment on the subtleties of what somebody is feeling. How might you use this information to increase your advantage when you're trying to spot if somebody is truthful? Begin by checking whether you can understand which feelings the person is going through. Try and get an idea of the feeling you think the person is having through his words, if the feelings being communicated are sure, odds are, you won't make an accurate judgment. Instead, turn the discussion to increasingly pessimistic encounters, and after that see whether you think the person is telling the truth.

Difference between lying and deception

Our way of life makes an unusual similarity between lie and deceit. Accordingly, we have different sentiments about both ideas. One is thought of as "wrong," while the other is to a great extent endured.

To lie is to put forth a false expression with the goal to cheat, at the end of the day, lying is all about saying something that isn't valid. To deceive, on the other hand, is "to make someone accept what is false or invalid." In both cases, the victim believes something that isn't valid.

Lying is a type of trickery, while deception does not generally include lying.

The main difference between lying and deception can be found in the detail. Did you state something that isn't valid? It's safe to say that at that point, you lied. In any case, if you suggest something that wasn't valid, you didn't lie.

Deception techniques

The "Land of Is" Technique

Most questions need a yes or no answer. At the point when someone doesn't have any desire to answer yes or no, they regularly go to what is known as the Land of Is. The Land of Is can be known as the thin line between truth and deception. The Land of Is comprises of misleading statements, suspicions, and verbal judo. The vast majority need to come clean, so they put forth an attempt to twist the facts to keep up with the lies without letting it be known. People always end up in the Land of Is, and they never know it.

To test people to spot if they are lying, ask a yes or no question. On the off chance that they fail to answer yes or no, a warning should spring up. After somebody gives a tangled response to a question, ask once more. If the person fails to reply with a yes or no, there is a chance that the person is trying to deceive you.

The "Well" Answer

If you ask somebody a yes or no question, and you get an answer that starts with "Well," there is a chance that person is telling a lie. At the point when a person answers with "Well," it shows that the person is going to give an answer he thinks you are not anticipating.

How to be of Deceptive at Work

Building trust at work can be a tricky thing. With co-workers, your boss, and the people you just meet. There are very distinct signs to tell for sure though if someone at the office or in your work environment is deceitful. Here are some common behavior traits:

❖ **Morphing stories**

Someone who exaggerates or underestimates their stories is someone that is trying to hide something. For example, if you hear someone tell the same story, but the details are different each time. This someone is trying to hide that they weren't really sick that day. Or they are not so good at what they keep bragging that they are about.

❖ Gossiper

When someone gossips in the office about another person, you can be sure that you are their next target. This person makes it evident that they cannot be trusted, as it is a breach of privacy. When you see this happening either leave the office or continue to listen so you can learn how to "gossip" better. Learn what not to do and figure out just how to be discreet when telling secrets. Try out of the office for example.

❖ A prominent flake.

Ever been around someone who makes promises they don't keep? Or say things they don't act upon? This is a flake. If you want to be a better deceptionist than this person, maybe renege a couple of times. Remember, the goal is to gain trust so you can form a bond. Once the bond is formed, your excuses and flaking won't seem to be that big of a deal as they are under your spell.

❖ Name dropper

We all have been around that colleague who likes to blame specific people that may or may not have had anything to do with a situation. This is name dropping. To be good at this, get people hyped about a scenario or situation and then name the "who shall not be named" making it clear you would never drop names of others because it's "rude." Knowing full well, that is precisely what you are doing. Not only will people succumb to wanting to know more, but they will also fall for the demise you're trying to create. Making others think you are a good person will make them become drawn to you. Secrets are not made to be mentioned. Including yours.

CHAPTER 9

HYPNOTISM UTILIZATION

Hypnosis is a cooperative interaction (or supposed to be a cooperative interaction) in which the participant responds to being entranced by the hypnotist. Hypnotism is used for all aspects of life. It is a form of getting into the mind, taking out the bad and replacing it with good. Or the other way around if you have dark intentions. Hypnosis is proven to reduce signs of anxiety and pain in patients with these illnesses.

The Four Stages of Hypnosis

Stage 1: Absorb Attention

This involves an attack on personality, which involves ideas like, "You are not who you think you are," a deliberate assault on the character or inner self of the victim. The operator denies everything that makes the identity of the person with statements like, "You are not a warrior." "You are not a man," and, "You are not guarding opportunity." To absorb the attention of the victim, the brainwasher draws them in using their tonality, their physiology, and their reputation to ensure the hypnosis is successful.

Stage 2: Bypass the Critical Faculty

The critical faculty is the part of the mind that uses logic and reasoning. If you have watched or read something that confuses you, and you are sure that what you are imagining cannot be possible, this is critical faculty. The operator tries to bypass this so that the victim can respond in an unconscious state. However, if the client feels threatened in any way through the process, the critical faculty will switch back on resulting in breaking the trance.

Stage 3: Activate an Unconscious Response

An unconscious response is that of a person communicating on a level of unawareness. The victim is unaware that they are being hypnotized, and will have no recollection of what is happening or what has happened throughout the process. The offender will dive into the victim's mind and place or replace thoughts, beliefs, perceptions, and values of the victim by creating visualizations for the client.

Stage 4: Leading the Unconscious to the Desired Outcome

Once the victim has reached all three stages of the hypnotic state, hypnotic suggestions and metaphors can be used. Hypnotic suggestions are used in commands and can be used to create an immediate or posthypnosis effect. Metaphors are stories cautiously constructed to help the unconscious mind become resourceful.

The Outcome

When all four stages are completed successfully, the result in the client or victim becomes whatever the perpetrator has brainwashed, or hypnotized into their mind, resulting in either a positive outcome or a negative one, depending on who you are dealing with.

How Does Hypnosis Work

Don't listen to the stereotypical point of view about hypnotism. It does not consist of a guy swinging a pocket watch in front of your face while saying phrases in a monotone voice. The hypnotist's job is to serve as a coach or trainer to help the client become hypnotized. Hypnotism is a state characterized by focused attention, heightened sensibility, and vivid fantasies. While a person is in the hypnotic state, they may come off as sleep or zoned out. In actuality, they are in a state of super high awareness. Hypnotherapists use visualization and verbal repetition to induce the hypnotic state.

The purpose for hypnosis is to get an individual to open up their mind to what they have buried deeper than the surface. The hypnotic state allows people to explore painful thoughts, feelings, and memories that are rather hard for them to bare consciously. Hypnotism is a treatment for sufferers to get them to perceive things differently. There are two ways hypnosis is used, suggestion therapy and analysis.

Suggestion Therapy

The client will be able to respond better to suggestions. This helps them change their behaviors such as to quit smoking or nail-biting. Suggestion therapy is very helpful with people who suffer chronic pain by changing the way they perceive sensations.

Analysis

This approach is used on people that suffer from mood, PTSD, and anxiety disorders. The analysis gets the client to a relaxed state so the hypnotist can find the psychological root of the problem. Once the problem is revealed, it can be addressed in psychotherapy.

How to Hypnotize Someone

It is easy to hypnotize a willing patient because in reality, they are actually hypnotizing themselves which is known as self-hypnosis. Your job as the hypnotist is to guide them into a relaxed state to fall into a waking sleep. This method is one of the easiest because you need no experience and can be used on the willing. This is called the progressive relaxation method.

Step One: Prepare

1. **Find a willing participant to practice on.**

If your participant doesn't want to be hypnotized, this can make things very difficult. You must find someone who is willing and believes it will work. Do not try to hypnotize someone with a history of mental disorders. It can lead to unintended consequences for that person.

2. Choose a safe and quiet place.

The environment has to have a relaxing vibe, so your client will be able to relax. Set the mood. This consists of dimming the lights and having a nice smelling surrounding. Have them sit in a comfortable chair and remove any distractions. This could be things like the TV, or putting the dog outside and the kids to bed. It should be just the two of you together. Be aware that cell phones should be turned off, windows should be closed, and letting people know that you are busy and not to be bothered.

3. Explanations.

Let the participant know what to expect and make sure they know the consequences. Maybe do some research together before starting, so that there are no misconceptions. As we have seen on TV and other series, most people may think too much into the stereotypes of hypnotism. It is best to let your client know that these are mythical, tell them the facts. Let them know they are not asleep or unconscious, they are not under a spell, and they will not do anything they don't want to do.

Step Two: Induce the Tranced State

1. Communicate in a low, slow, soothing voice.

Take your time when vocalizing to the participant. Your voice has to be smooth and calm. Draw out your sentences being careful not to put emphasis on them. When you are in the process of relaxing the participant, imagine you are trying to calm a frightened or worried person. It is best to keep a steady tone throughout the entire process.

Some words to start with can be, "Let my words settle you and take the suggestions as you wish," "You are safe. Everything is peaceful. Please sink into your chair and relax," "Your eyes are feeling heavy. Let your body relax. Listen to my body being aware of your muscles as you become more relaxed," and, "You are in complete control. Accept the suggestions given that only you are willing to benefit from."

2. Ask them to breathe deeply and slowly.

Using the same tone and concentration, ask them to breathe through their nose and out through their mouths. Ask them to pay attention to which part of the body they feel most of the oxygen coming from. It's like teaching them step by step how to breathe and focus their minds on just breathing. Let them know this is their only obligation, to just breathe. Make it important that the surroundings are calm and safe, and if their mind wanders to bring their attention back to the breath.

3. Focus their gaze.

Ask them to open their eyes if they are closed, unless they want to keep them closed, and focus on something. It can be your forehead, or something dimly lit. Once they have fixated on an object, ask them to focus intensely on this object, not looking away. Also, let them know it is okay to keep their eyes closed. If you notice that they are struggling to keep their eyes still, give them guidance, telling them to focus on something specific.

4. Get them to relax every inch of their body.

Once you notice your participant is calm and relaxed. Remind them to continue to breathe slowly. Now it is time to ask them to relax their toes and feet. Once they have done this carefully taking in a breath after relaxing their feet, move to the next muscle group. Ask them to relax their legs and calves, to their stomach, chest and back, and next to their arms and hands. Finally, ask them to relax the muscles on their shoulders, neck, and head. Take as much time as you need, and let them know they can take time as well. It is important not to rush.

5. Calm them further.

Make your voice repetitive at this stage. Tell them that with every word you whisper they are slowly sinking deeper and deeper into relaxation. Make it known that they are staying completely aware, yet completely relaxed. Reassure them that they are safe and then repeat the words "You are sinking deeper into relaxation now." If you notice their eyes are darting or they are subtly fidgeting, just focus their attention back to their breath. Reteach them to breathe slowly and deeply.

6. Visually create the relaxation staircase.

Tell your participant to picture a staircase that has ten steps. Tell them that with each step they walk down, their body gets lighter and their tension becomes no more. With every step down the stairs, they are taking in another deep breath. The goal is when they reach the bottom they are to be in full subconscious mode.

Step Three: Using Hypnosis to Help

1. Understand that tricking someone in this state usually doesn't work and is a trust violation.

Most people will remember their experience and be upset if you try to fool them. If you don't know what you are doing, then your good intentions can lead to bad results. The goal is to help your participant in letting go of their problems and life stresses.

2. Ask them to imagine solutions to their current problems.

Instead of telling the participant what to do or think, ask them to solve their own problems. Do this by telling them to imagine what their life is like in ten years from now, five years from now, a year from now and finally, a week from now. Ask them to picture all their problems and stresses that they are dealing with and then ask them to find the solution. Say things like, "What does success look like for you?" "How do you get there?" and "What do you want most from now to a month from now?" Ask them simple questions, but spin it positively.

3. Know that hypnosis is used for a variety of afflictions.

It is good to keep in your own mind that you are not a professional, and you won't be able to solve their issues. Understand the fact that hypnosis has been used for addiction, pain relief, phobias, self-esteem issues, and others. Unless guided by a hypnotist, you should stick to the basics. Ask the individual to imagine a day without smoking. Whatever they suffer from the most, ask them to picture a life with or without it to help them see there is a benefit.

Final Step Four: Ending the Session:

1. Slowly take them out of this state.

The last thing you want to do is alarm them out of the relaxation. Tell them the session is finished and to listen carefully to the instructions on how to come back. Let them know they are becoming aware of their surroundings. Ask your client to walk back up the stairs, back to where they came from. Once at the top of the stairs ask them to listen to what is around them, say they can move their toes and fingers. Finally, make them aware that once you count to five they can open their eyes and they will be fully alert. Then count to five slowly.

2. Discuss the hypnosis.

Go over what it was like for them so you can gain insight on how to improve. Ask them how they felt, and what they went through. Ask them what they enjoyed and did not enjoy. If they don't feel like talking, it is okay to give them time to talk about it later.

CHAPTER 10

DARK SEDUCTION PSYCHOLOGY

Seduction is a process in which a person deliberately entices another person to get what they want in a sexual manner. Someone seduces another person because they want a relationship, to lead astray, to feel righteous. An offender can use seduction to corrupt or persuade sexual activity for a pleasurable benefit. Strategies include almost all of what we have learned in this book, such as nonverbal communication (NLP), deception, persuasion, short-term behavioral tactics, and enticing body language. If seduction is used negatively, it involves temptation and enticement to lead someone astray into a behavioral choice they wouldn't have made if they weren't in sexual arousal.

The Techniques Used in Dark Seduction

Sometimes, seduction has nothing to do with sex, but it's the game surrounding temptation. It's getting someone to become aroused for the sake of having their minds want what the offender wants. Seduction is another meaning for anticipation. Someone can be anticipated for anything such as a vacation or getting a new pet. It's the desire behind the temptation that has people searching and exploring their needs to get what they want. Continue reading for some tactics on how to use seduction negatively.

❖ **Choose the right victim.**

As explained throughout this book, you have now learned how to get to know someone thoroughly. Choosing someone who is susceptible to your charms is the best victim. This type of person has to be isolated, or unhappy and can easily be enticed into doing as you please. The perfect victim is someone who can be chased because your seductive measures will seem more natural and dynamic.

❖ **Create a sense of security—falsely.**

The offender should begin to seduce indirectly so that the target gradually becomes aware of you. If the perpetrator is direct too early, they risk stirring up resistance that will become impossible to get lower. It is best to approach the victim precariously through a third-party moving from friend to lover with their target. Once the victim feels secure and that they can trust you, that is when you strike.

❖ **Send mixed signals.**

Once the victim is aware and intrigued by you, you need to stimulate their interest before they move their attention elsewhere. Sending mixed messages like being harsh, then soft—both spiritual and earthly, innocent and cunning. The reason for this technique is because mixed signals can lead to the depth of a person. With wisdom comes intrigue and fascination. The target will be confused yet want to know more. To get the best result for this, you must create power by hinting at something contradictory within yourself.

❖ **Appear to be an object of desire.**

If you have attracted interest beyond other people, then you are most likely going to attract your target. People who fail to draw the attention of others fail in the temptation process. Create an aura of desirability to achieve the goal of attraction. If you are a trendsetter or the focus of attention, many people will want to "win" you over and take you away from the crowd of admirers.

❖ **Create a need—mix anxiety and discontentment.**

163

If you are trying to seduce a perfectly satisfied person, it will not work. To get the target to anticipate temptation with you, they must be tense and unrested. If they are on the brink of this or can be easily manipulated, you must instill feelings of discontent in them. Pain and anxiety are the perfect preconditions to pleasure.

❖ **Master insinuation**

If your target feels dissatisfied and relies on you to meet their attention, then this is crucial to seducing them. If you are too obvious in your tricks, then you will be left with no victim as they will run from you. Insinuation consists of planting a seed inside the mind of the target. So to drop a hint, then days later they have it appear as if it was their idea is how insinuation works best. To do this, the offender says something bold followed by a retraction and an apology, evasive comments, and small talk combined with alluring glances.

❖ **Create temptation.**

By creating temptation, you can easily lure your victim into your trap. Awake the desire in your targets so that they want more, and they cannot control themselves. Find their weakness and exploit it. Show them their fantasies can come to life. Stimulate curiosity stronger than doubt and anxiety that goes with the unknown.

❖ **Keep them guessing.**

If you make it known what to expect from you, then the spell will be broken. By creating suspense, it keeps the victim on point, always guessing whats next. This keeps them intrigued and wanting more. People like to be spontaneous, whether they like to admit that or not, so surprising them will give them a sense of spontaneity. Just as you are heading one way, change direction giving the victim thrill and excitement.

❖ **Pay attention to detail.**

Thoughtful gifts made just for them, clothes, jewelry, or anything designed to please them will have them mesmerized by you. If you shower them with the attention they don't normally get, then they will continue to stay your prize. Doing this shows them that you pay attention to their needs and give them what they want. Little do they know it's a setup for getting what you so desire.

❖ Poeticize your presence.

When an offender leaves their victim alone for too long, their victim will become distant. If a target thinks their offender is not around, the game is over. The trick is to remain elusive. Create memories through objects. Associate yourself with images and nonverbal actions. That way when the victim lives their lives when the perpetrator is busy, the victim can envelop the offender in their fantasies when they think or see something that reminds them of their person.

❖ Disarm through weaknesses and vulnerability.

Put the shoe on the other foot. Your perfect target is weak and vulnerable. Up to this point they are enthralled by you. It's time to turn the tables. You need to strategize how you portray your weaknesses and vulnerabilities. This is to make them feel superior like they want to help you and engage with your emotions. This will also make them feel like you are opening up and your actions will seem more natural. Play the victim, then transform the subject's sympathy into love.

❖ Mix pleasure with pain.

The worst thing someone can do while trying to seduce is to be too kind. If the offender works too hard, they will come off as insecure and monotonous. When things start to get good, inflict the target with pain. Make them feel guilty and create the illusion of a breakup. When they are feeling helpless and cry out for the need of you again, return to being nice and you will have them. The lower the blows, the higher the make-up will be. To excite the seduction, create fear.

By becoming what someone needs at the time, and then forcing a whirlwind of distraction, confusion, the ups, and the downs, you will become their biggest fantasy. Careful not to overdo anything, and plan out your moves strategically. The minute someone feels they are being played, it's game over.

Why People Use Seduction

People use seductions for many reasons such as getting ahead in their career, moving to the next stage in a relationship and getting something they want for a deal. Manipulators use seduction for personal benefits and pleasure. Seduction is something that can be dangerous, or very harmless. The choice is yours. Here is what you will need to contain seduction successfully.

❖ **Desire**

Awakening the desire, in the target of interest is key to temptation. Desire is much like ambition. Go after what you want because you want it so badly. Overcoming the fear of failure will help you become successful in fulfilling this trait. The idea of desire is to keep the anticipation of what's next to come. The answer is never a no, but a possible yes, or a maybe. Keep the victim guessing leaving them wanting more. Trigger emotional buttons in people, and you will master the art of seduction.

❖ **Confidence**

You can't seduce someone if you don't have the confidence to know you can. So in short, without confidence comes no temptation. The key to confidence is trusting yourself. If you trust yourself, then you can trust that there are lots to love about you. If you like yourself, then insecurities can't get in your head. Confident people's aura shows that they are happy to be who they are. Hence, confident people will usually get what they want. Fake it until you make it is often what is said. This means if you are not something that you want to be, fake it and it shall become real over time.

❖ Arousal

Find out what makes someone vulnerable and play on that emotion. This will awaken their arousal. The goal is to get in touch with your skills. What makes you so intriguing? When you can answer this for yourself, you will be able to show this answer to someone else. Thus, they will lust you, and you will have succeeded in opening their arousal.

Master these three elements, and you will become the master charmer. When you build a connection with people, you can exploit their resources and affection to get what you want in the end. When you achieve the role in temptation, then you will be more confident. Confidence leads to greater success through life. See where I am going with this?

CHAPTER 11

PSYCHOLOGICAL WARFARE

Psychological Warfare is the planned tactical use of publicity, threats, and other noncombat techniques during wars, or periods of conflict. The purpose was to mislead, intimidate, demoralize, or influence the behavior and thoughts of the enemy. To be successful in the army's objectives, the planners of psychological warfare (PSYWAR) campaigns, they gained complete knowledge of the enemy's beliefs, likes and dislikes, strengths and weaknesses, and vulnerabilities. This was so they could win the war.

Other names for PSYWAR are MISO, PSYOP (psychological operations), "hearts and minds," and propaganda. Various techniques are used to stimulate confessions or reinforce attitudes and behaviors to the originator's objectives. Target audiences are not just limited to soldiers, but governments, companies, groups, and individuals.

 In early psychological warfare, soldiers would beat their swords against their shields as a sign to threaten or instill fear in their opponents. In the 525 BC Battle of Peluseium, Persian forces would hold cats hostage to gain leverage over the Egyptians because of the religious beliefs they had—not to harm cats. In the thirteenth century AD, the Mongolian Empire leader made his troops carry three lit torches at a time as a means to make his army look bigger. To frighten villagers, the Mongol armies would catapult human heads over village walls.

In modern psychological warfare, during World War I, technological advances made it easier for government systems to distribute propaganda through mass-circulation newspapers. During World War II, Hitler's rise to power was driven by propaganda in Germany, designed to discredit his political opponents. His angry speeches compiled national pride while convincing villagers to blame others for Germany's self-induced economic problems.

Techniques and Methods

Psychological Warfare is a method that uses fear and uncertainty to break down the mental and emotional well-being of an opponent. Here is a list of techniques that are used:

1. News Outlets

The news is an information panel that almost everyone sees or reads. The press can run whatever information it chooses, whether it's government-run or independently owned. A population could be tainted or brainwashed by paying attention to the news. Most of the time the story happens to be correct, and so it is a viable source people will listen to.

2. Threats

Whether they be empty threats or actual—threats of violence, restriction of freedom, and control—is made to instill fear in people or organizations. Constant warnings can damage a group or individuals psychological state resulting in anxiety and terror.

3. Leaflets

Leaflets are pieces of paper dropped by air forces over war territories that have manipulative messages or pictures written on them. The goal is to get the opponent to surrender or fight the political event taking place.

4. Objects

Objects are souvenirs like T-shirts, posters, hats, pins, and so on. This is another effective way to get a message or point across. The objects can become symbols for more prominent correspondence regarding politics, beliefs, religious philosophies, etc. They are used for worship and promotion.

5. False Flag

A false flag is an empty threat or a message that consists of a lie to instill concern or dread in people. The blame is put on a different organization to gain control and shift attention.

6. Media

Media is a discreet way to get in our head through subliminal messages. Films, music, and books are tools for psychological warfare. The media can form a new perspective and put ideas in the minds of the population.

7. Demoralization

Demoralization consists of direct transmission through publications or radio, books, and pamphlets, delivery systems like airplane drops, smuggling, and deception. Demoralization in the context of PSYWAR is the objective to weaken morale among enemy combatants. This encourages the opponent to retreat, surrender, or fight rather than defeating them on the battlefield.

CHAPTER 12

CASE STUDIES

Some case studies in this chapter are considered wrong and ruthless. Before reading or listening, be advised that some of the content matter may be offensive or derogative. These are dark examples of experiments used by psychologists and scientists. There are many more case studies than what is written here, but these are to get you to understand the different ways dark psychology has come about. Many of these experiments have a hidden meaning regardless of the intention of the projects. Enjoy.

Wild Boy of Aveyron

The "Wild Boy of Aveyron" named Victor lived in the forest of Aveyron for several years in the 1800s. He was age eleven or twelve. After he had been spotted leaving the forest of Aveyron, psychologists and philosophers studied him naming him the "natural experiment." This is how the question nature versus nurture came to life. When Victor was brought into civilization, he was dirty and tousled. Food was something that largely motivated him. When he was transported to Paris and Itard, the cities began a mission to teach the boy how to socialize and become a part of society. The program was slightly successful, but not quite. Victor never learned to speak fluently, but he learned how to dress and use the washroom. He learned how to write and acquired basic comprehension. Scientists will never know his background but have theories revolving around autism. Autism expert Uta Frith believed that Victor got abandoned because he may have had autism. Because of this case, the boy has been an inspiration throughout history. A 2004 novel called The Wild Boy was published and was dramatized in the 1970 French film called The Wild Child.

H. M.

Henry Molaison died in 2008, goes by H. M. to protect his privacy to the public. He had severe amnesia as age twenty-seven after having brain surgery for treatment from epilepsy. Over 100 psychologists and neurologists studied him and had been mentioned in twelve thousand or more journal articles. Molaison's surgery involved removing a large part of the hippocampus part of the brain on both sides. The result was that he lost almost all of his long-term memory. Considering researchers and scientists studied that only the cerebral cortex was to blame for memory loss, this brain surgery was quite the popular focus. Molaison's brain was carefully sliced and preserved which is now turned into a 3-D digital atlas.

Anna O.

Anna O. is a pseudonym for Bertha Pappenheim, who died in 1936 age seventy-seven. She was a German Jewish feminist and social worker. As Anna O, she is known as one of the first patients ever to undergo psychoanalysis, and her case inspired Freud's thoughts on mental illness. Joseph Breuer, a psychoanalyst, was brought to her house in Vienna, where he witnesses her lying in her bed entirely paralyzed. Some symptoms she had experienced was hallucinations, personality changes, and rambling speech, in which doctors found no physical cause. Breuer visited her almost every day for eighteen months and talked to her. They spoke of her thoughts and feelings, including her grief for her father, and what seemed to be the most interesting was that the more she talked, the more her symptoms would fade. Researchers had named this the "talking cure," first ever instances revolving psychoanalysis. In the later days of Pappenheim's life, she had become a productive writer which she included authoring stories, plays, and translation. She founded social clubs for Jewish women and the German Federation of Jewish Women. She also worked in orphanages.

Little Albert

Little Albert was the nickname for John Watson; a behaviorist psychologist had given to an eleven-month-old baby. John Watson alongside his fiancé Rosalind Rayner deliberately attempted to instill specific fears in the child through a process called conditioning. The results were documented in 1920 and had become notorious for being the most unethical procedure ever done. A few years later, an academic quarrel had erupted over Little Albert's true identity. A group led by Hall Beck confirmed in 2011 that Little Albert's real name was Douglas Meritte, the son of a wet nurse (a woman employed to breastfeed another woman's child) at John Hopkins University—where Watson and his fiancé were based. Based on this knowledge, that would mean sadly that Little Albert died at the age of six because of a condition called hydrocephalus (fluid in the brain). However, this knowledge was challenged by a different group led by Russel Powell. Their theory was that Little Albert actual name was William A Barger (recorded in his medical files as Albert Barger) the son of a different wet nurse. Later in the year 2015, textbook writer confirmed that the second theory was more credible. If this is true, that would mean that Little Albert died at age eighty-seven in 2007.

Chris Sizemore

Chris Sizemore is most famous for having been diagnosed with multiple personality disorder, known today as a dissociative identity disorder. Sizemore's alter egos names were Eve White, Eve Black, Jane, and multiple others. Sizemore expressed these personalities as a coping mechanism for her traumatic childhood. She said she had witnessed her man being beaten and saw a man sawn in half. Later in Sizemore's life, she mentioned that her alter egos were combined into one. She had explained that Eve White was the mother of her first child and that Eve White was married to her husband and she wasn't. Later, her story was turned into a movie in 1957 called The Three Faces of Eve. In 1977, Sizemore published her autobiography called I'm Eve, and in 2009, she appeared on the BBC's Hard Talk interview series.

David Reimer

Reimer lost his penis in a circumcision operation when he was eight months old. His parents were advised by a psychologist John Money to raise Reimer as a girl, so his parents renamed him Brenda. They set up plans and further surgery to get him to go through hormone treatment to assist a gender reassignment. The assignment was problematic because of Reimer's boyish personality and found out the truth about himself at age fourteen. Later, he campaigned against other children with genital injuries being gender reassigned the same way he had been. His story was turned into a book named As Nature Made Him: The Boy Who Was Raised as a Girl by John Colapinto. He is also the subject of two BBC horizon documentaries. Unfortunately, Reimer killed himself when he was thirty-eight years old in 2004.

Emma Eckstein

Sigmund Freud decided to use Eckstein for various experiments after she had asked him for help with stomach ailments and slight depression. Freud told Eckstein that she was being treated for hysteria and excessive masturbation repetitively. At that time, these two habits were known as mental illness. Freud gave Emma cocaine, and a local anesthetic before the inside of her nose was cauterized—a disastrous treatment. He continued to treat her with this for three years, and no one knows what his intentions were to this day.

Electroshock Therapy on Children

Dr. Lauretta Bender of the Creedmore Hospital in New York chose over one hundred young children to use electroshock therapy on based on her theoretic beliefs. Bender made her patients sit in front of a large group and applied pressure to their foreheads. Any child who slightly cringed or moved because of the pressure was thought to have early signs of schizophrenia. Bender believed electroshock therapy was the only treatment to solve this social issue. Her peers confirmed that they thought she had never shown sympathy for the children in her care. The youngest child to be worked on was three years old.

The Monster Study

In 1939, twenty-two orphans living in Davenport, Iowa, became test subjects of a couple named Wendell Johnson and Mary Tudor. The study consisted of speech impediments and stuttering. The children were split in half, into two groups. One group received positive speech therapy and were praised consistently on their speech. The other group received negative speech therapy. This included being belittled for any speech imperfection and violent consequences. The conclusion of the study was the children in the second, negative group developed speech problems throughout their lives and had never had imperfections before the experiment. The experiment was never published because Johnson and Tudor feared the comparisons people would believe of human experiments among the Nazis.

Project MK-Ultra

Project MK-Ultra was an experiment involving violent torture such as giving subject's mind-altering drugs, sensory deprivation, verbal and sexual abuse, extreme isolation and hypnosis. This experiment was meant to figure out the best ways to manipulate the mental states of American citizens. The project was funded and sponsored by the CIA and could find these experiments being done at prisons, hospitals, and universities. Luckily, Congress shut down Project MK-Ultra later in the year 1973. This experiment went on for twenty years starting in 1953.

The Monkey Drug Trials

A research facility began an unethical experiment on monkeys in 1969. They wanted to test the effects of drug addiction, so they trained a large number of monkeys on how to inject themselves with needles. The various drugs were morphine, alcohol, cocaine, nicotine, codeine, and amphetamines. When the monkeys learned how to inject themselves, they were left in a room with a significant supply of drugs lying around. The monkey went haywire. Their acts consisted of breaking limbs to escape the lab, pulling hair from a specific part of their bodies, and others mixed a bunch of drugs in which they died shortly after.

Facial Expressions Experiment

Carney Landis began an experiment to study common facial expression. He wanted to know if everyone had the same facial expression based on what they saw. The facial expressions he wanted to experiment with were happiness, shock, and disgust. To conduct his experiment, Landis recruited many participants and painted their facial lines black. He then exposed his participants to images and videos like pornography, ammonia, touching reptiles, and beheading rats. Once the participants had an expression, he would snap their photograph to save for his results. This happened in 1924.

Bobo Doll Experiment

In the 1960s, psychologist Albert Bandura wanted to test how children learn behaviors based on their influences. Bandura got a large doll named Bobo and had a percentage of seventy-two primary-aged children watch adults violently beat this doll. Then he left the children in a room alone with Bobo and observed what they would do. A large number of children also began to abuse the doll quite violently. Bandura repeated this experiment twice, and the results were the same.

Racism among Elementary School Students

Jane Elliott, a schoolteacher, experimented with her student to teach them about racism. Many outsiders judged her publicly for her teaching methods, and others had an issue with the fact that she was exposing white children to such measures. The experiment was successful and was perhaps a life lesson for all the students. In 1968, Martin Luther King Jr. had been assassinated, so while Elliott tried to explain racism to her children, she asked the students with blue eyes to go to one side of the room while the kids with brown stayed on the other side. The kids with blue eyes, she treated as a superior group and cited fake scientific studies claiming those with blue eyes were better. A week later, she switched groups and provided the same tactic with the ones with brown eyes. Elliott received public backlash because of this. But the method got the point across, and some may consider her a hero.

CONCLUSION

Finally, dark psychology will never disappoint when employed positively. If you got to the end of this book, there is no way back. Armed with this strength of knowledge, you should be ready to put dark art skills in practice at the office, in church, or at home in your relationships.

Simply follow the techniques discussed in the book, and you can easily persuade anyone. The application of dark psychology is a two-way street; you can stop the smooth criminal in their tracks because it now takes just a second to spot this deceptive person weaving their way into your mind and soul through peddling lies. Or you can choose to become the predator weaving your way into other people's lives.

The myths that have stood for ages have been shattered in this book; and this book clearly explains the skills used in the dark arts that the public previously thought was magic. Hypnotism, for instance, is a misunderstood science, but its benefits are numerous, and its utility can save lives.

The dark traits discussed here are living examples that we experience in everyday life and not mere illusions in a movie.

You can rest easy and cast your fears and doubts of dark psychology and begin the journey to becoming a better and skilled dark psychologist. Don't keep waiting anymore. Go ahead, put your skills into practice and implement what you have learnt.

www.ingramcontent.com/pod-product-compliance
Lightning Source LLC
Chambersburg PA
CBHW080557030426
42336CB00019B/3224